Prayers for All Seasons

Based on the
Revised Common Lectionary
Year A

Prayers for All Seasons

Based on the
Revised Common Lectionary
Year A

Wood Lake

Editor: Ellen Turnbull
Cover design: Cyrus Gandevia
Text design: Robert MacDonald
Proofreader: Dianne Greenslade

Library and Archives Canada Cataloguing in Publication
Prayers for all seasons : based on the revised Common lectionary year A.
Includes index.
Issued in print and electronic formats.
ISBN 978-1-77064-809-8 (paperback).—ISBN 978-1-77064-810-4 (html)
1. Prayers. 2. Lectionaries. I. Turnbull, Ellen, editor
BV245 P729 2016 264'.13 C2016-902846-1
C2016-902847-X

ISBN 978-1-77064-809-8

Published by Wood Lake Publishing Inc.
485 Beaver Lake Road, Kelowna, BC, Canada, V4V 1S5
www.woodlake.com | 250.766.2778

We acknowledge the financial support of the Government of Canada. Nous reconnaissons l'appui financier du gouvernement du Canada. Wood Lake Publishing acknowledges the financial support of the Province of British Columbia through the Book Publishing Tax Credit.

Printed in Canada.
Printing 10 9 8 7 6 5 4 3 2 1

CONTENTS

CONTENTS

SEASON OF ADVENT

Advent 1

(Year A begins on the First Sunday of Advent in 2016, 2019, 2022…)

LECTIONARY READINGS
Isaiah 2:1–5
Psalm 122
Romans 13:11–14
Matthew 24:36–44

God of holy peace, may our Advent prayers for your coming be linked with Advent lives that follow your leading. Transform our implements of death-dealing into tools for life-giving. May we attend to prophets, old and new, who bid us toward you. Amen.

***

Each week in Advent a prophetic voice can call the people to remember the promises of God. The person speaking should not be seen by the congregation but the voice needs to be clearly heard.

Listen to the hope of God!
Listen to the hope of God,
in the noise of life around us.

It is hope that fills children with life,
and brings fullness to the laughter of neighbours.
Can you hear it?

It is hope that fills the voice with the shout of justice,
and makes freedom a restless cause.
This is hope.

It is hope that moves the preaching of God's word to the living of it,
and helps prayer become a way of life.

This is hope.

I recognize hope in the braying of animals –
in the bleating of sheep and the roar of lions,
in the growl of the bear and the bark of the badger –
all living together in peace.
Can you hear them?
This is hope.

Come, listen and live in this hope.

***

Invite people to cup their hands during this prayer and imagine holding the promise of Advent.

God of promises, we gather in expectation, wondering about this season and recognizing the longing within us for all your promises to be filled full. As we wait for your coming, may we shape a space for you this Advent, creating a time and a place to hear your word for our lives. May our time together now be one of renewal as we listen to the good news of your reign of peace in this world. Amen.

***

One: On each Sunday of Advent, we light one candle, illuminating God's truth: hope in the midst of all that frightens us, all that is unknown, all that keeps us lonely. Soon, just a few weeks from now, all four candles will burn brightly, and we will know that Christmas has come. We respond with the words of Isaiah 2:5. Until then, we wait, and we walk together along the path of Advent.

Today we light the candle for hope. God promised God's people that a leader would rise up among us – but that it would be a different kind of leader, and a different kind of power. Even with growling beasts all around, a child leads the way.

All: **Just as the sun endures, may God's light burn without end!**

Two: God tells us of a coming power that will be a paradox, not always easy for us to understand, but we are assured that the hope of Advent lies in trusting a truth that will set all of us free, predators and prey alike.

All: **Come, let us walk in the light of the Lord!**

***

Spirit of Christ, in your coming
you want to shape us into a people
of hope, peace, joy, and love.

But we confess that instead of hope,
we allow cynicism to shape us and
we mould for ourselves shields
of biting humour and noisy alarms
to protect our hearts and hurts.

Instead of peace,
we allow fear to shape us and
we mould for ourselves weapons
of pre-emptive violence
to protect our homes and our homeland.

Instead of joy,
we allow worry to shape us and
we mould for ourselves bombs
wired by the dream of deterrence
to protect our fortunes and futures.

Instead of love,
we allow anger to shape us and
we mould for ourselves the guns
of justified aggression
to protect our bullet-riddled souls.

O Spirit of Christ,
help us to see the ways we have allowed

fear, cynicism, worry, and anger to shape us
instead of your way of graceful shalom.
(silent reflection)

***

God takes all that we are,
and all our world has become,
and reshapes our fear, cynicism, worry, and anger
into peace, hope, joy, and love. For God knows that in everything
something new can appear.
Our weapons of destruction can become tools of fruitfulness,
our cynical minds can become fertile with hope,
our anxious hearts can become filled with your joy,
our words of hurt can become acts of love.
This is the power of God's love among us
and we are remoulded, reshaped, re-created by God's own hand.
Praise be to you, O God. Amen.

***

Holy Spirit of Peace,
in a world of war, seen and unseen,
in a time of trouble and trauma,
we dare say, we dare imagine, we dare confess:
Yours is the kin-dom, the power, and the glory.
Open your ancient words for us.
Help our souls imagine your new vision for us. Amen.

Advent 2

LECTIONARY READINGS

Isaiah 11:1–10
Psalm 72:1–7, 18–19
Romans 15:4–13
Matthew 3:1–12

Lead us, O God, to hope. Lead us to hope by the power of your Spirit, as we allow your Spirit to shape us. Lead us to hope with the trusting hand of a child, as we would learn anew from children what it means to trust. Amen.

***

Listen!
Listen to the stirring of the heavens.
The stars are gathering,
the light shifts,
and there is a steady beat, beat, beat
across the universe.

Listen!
Listen to the rhythm of Advent.
A readying,
pulsing heartbeat,
steady and real beats, beats, beats,
across this season.

Listen!
Listen to the beat.
God's Advent beat,
transforming swords into ploughshares,
missiles to Communion plates,
rifles to rocking chairs.

Listen!
Come with me,

and pick up the beat of God.
For God is beating out the rhythm of something new.

***

God, who comes as a child, we gather to see you and know you today.
In this Advent season, as we gather once again to prepare for the miracle of your coming,
help us enter your paradox together.
Help us see the ultimate strength in the ultimate vulnerability.
Help us see how least is most, how the teeth-gnashing predatory world we so often experience is never your last word.
Open us to your logic-defying love this day, as we grow nearer to celebrating the Christ child bursting forth into the world.
In the paradox of life we pray. Amen.

***

One: *(while candles are being lit)* On this second Sunday of Advent, we light two candles, illuminating God's truth. Our first candle was for hope. Today, our second light is for peace – a sign to us that in a world of war, God lifts up a different way for us, inviting all to lay down our weapons of all kinds and pick up the tools for building peace.
All: **Come, let us walk in the light of the Lord!**

***

Bring this statement to life by inviting the children to lead the congregation in making the animal sound for every animal mentioned. If possible, divide the congregation in half and have each side make one of the noises in each line.

When the mouse *(squeak)* and the lion *(roar)* become friends,
God's peace becomes real.
When the snake *(hiss)* and the lamb *(baa)* live together,
God's peace becomes real.
When the dog *(woof)* and the cat *(meow)* share the same home,

God's peace becomes real.
When the rabbit *(wiggle nose)* and the coyote *(howl)* walk together,
God's peace becomes real.
When the donkey *(hee haw)* and the blackbird *(caw)* play together,
God's peace becomes real.
When the monkey *(chatter chatter)* and the tiger *(roar)* eat together,
God's peace becomes real.
When you *(point to someone)* and I *(point to self)* grow together,
God's peace becomes real.

***

Listening, Loving God, we lay down before you all the ways we have been growling and gruesome to each other. We lay down before you all the ways we have failed to stand up to predators, failed to defend helpless prey. While your cycle of life in creation is beautiful, we hear in your sacred word that you do not intend for us to bite and snarl at one another. You do not intend for us to look at one another and cry, "Predator!" Help us, Holy One. Help us see with your eyes, help us see how each of us can be predator and each of us can be prey. Help us not to see entire nations, entire peoples, as predators. Help us see as you see – that we are all part of one body.

Hear now, spoken aloud or in the silence of our hearts, the people and places which are in aching need of your healing and love.

God, we do not want to hurt or destroy. Hear our prayer. Make us the willing hands for the words we lift up today. In the name of the little child who leads us we pray. Amen.

***

As long as the sun burns in the sky,
God is the warm love between us.
As long as the tides of the ocean ebb and flow,
God is the constant peace in our lives.
As long as the mountains stand and the plains spread wide,
we will live the love and peace of God in our world.

You are the sprig of hope,
the shoot of promise bursting forth in our day;
go to enliven the realm of God's peace.

Blue Christmas Service

O God, keep faith with us this day.
Whether we are walking near your light,
or we are far away on a path of shadows,
make us aware of your steadfast love.
We know this is a season of growing light and joy,
yet it can be a time when our sorrows and pain
are harshly illumined in our hearts.
May we cling to the hope that, one day,
we will know the eternal happiness that is found in you.

***

Based on Psalm 80
O Great Creator,
who made the stars that shine in the night sky,
touch us with the gentle brush strokes of your love.
Restore us, Holy One; shine upon us that we may be made whole.
You who hovered over the waters of the deep,
meet us in the chaos of our varied lives.
Restore us, Holy One; shine upon us that we may be made whole.
You, who lived on earth as one of us,
knowing pain and suffering, laughter and joy,
are present now, in the midst of us as we pray.
Restore us, Holy One; shine upon us that we may be made whole.

***

We look for ways to flee your presence, ways to run from the pain, the disappointment, and the anger that remind us how much we really want love to define us. Help us, O God, to feel ourselves to be still in your presence, to know ourselves knit together from the inside, and to believe our worlds will stop unravelling. Amen.

***

You are fearfully and wonderfully made. Sisters and brothers, God's grace is that even in the fear, there is wonder.

***

Holy One,
gather up all the thoughts and prayers,
longings and tears
that we have offered this evening.
We entrust them to your safekeeping.

Gather up also the prayers
of all those we haven't named,
and don't even know,
who are hurting at this time.

We hold in your holy light the days and nights that lie ahead.
Steady us, guide us, and sustain us.
Keep us alert to the possibility of a miracle
breaking into our lives.

***

Offer each person a few glow-in-the-dark stars to take with them and place somewhere where they will see them at night and remember this time together.

May we be gentle with ourselves.
Remember that we are created in the image of God.
May we go into the world with honesty and thanksgiving,
embracing tears, laughter, and all that is good.
May the protection of God comfort us,
may the courage of Jesus sustain us,
may the tenderness of the Spirit embrace us. Amen.

Advent 3

LECTIONARY READINGS

Isaiah 35:1–10
Psalm 146:5–10 *or* Luke 1:47–55
James 5:7–10
Matthew 11:2–11

Liberating God, help us to know the insurrection you birthed in the form of a baby. As we are inspired by a young woman's humble, joyful obedience, remind us how you steer our lives, no matter how our ego struggles for control. May we hear your Advent call for revolution in our lives. Amen.

***

I have heard the voice of God
and it is calling to us through the wilderness.
From across the desert it summons us
to a highway, a path through the outback.

Where a desert once laid, God promises meadows.
Where a barren land once loomed, a fertile field will grow.
Where stark colours once blinded our eyes,
we will now rejoice in a glory of colour
and a festival of rainbows.

This is our transport journey: the Holy Way.
It will be like no other roadway ever built;
made of blossom and not tar, wild petals and not brick,
we will walk on it together.

I have heard the voice of God
and I am going to walk the way.
Come with me, my people.
Come with me into God's promised future.

***

Adapted from Luke 1:47–55

One: Our souls magnify the Most High

All: **and our spirits rejoice in God our Saviour.**

One: God's mercy is for those who love and revere God, from generation to generation.

All: **God has brought down the powerful from their thrones, and lifted up the lowly.**

One: God has filled the hungry with good things, and sent the rich away empty.

All: **Blessed be God's name. Let us worship God!**

***

One: On this third Sunday of Advent, we light three candles, illuminating God's truth. Our first candle was for hope, and the second was for peace. Today, our third candle is for joy. From prophets like Isaiah and Mary, we hear God's promises: the blind shall see, the deaf shall hear, the lame shall leap.

All: **We say to those with fearful hearts, "Do not fear! Here is your God!"** *(Isaiah 35:4)*

Two: *(Read while candles are being lit.)* God's promises sometimes seem impossible, and because we are human, we doubt. But the promises burn with everlasting light. Today, even in an unsteady world, may we find new ways to look into the light of Advent and rejoice that God's promises are true for each one of us and all of us.

All: **Come, let us walk in the light of the Lord!** *(Isaiah 2:5)*

***

When we have no good word to say, forgive us.
When our words for the world are barren and hard as rock,
when what we say to ourselves and to others does not contain the realm of love,
hear us as we confess.
In our barren living hear us and bring us to life once more.

When we live without sharing, forgive us.
When our actions are dry and without your intent,
when we live as if we do not hold your grace or contain your blessing for the world,
hear us as we confess.
In our dry living hear us and bring us to life once more.

When we live without joy, forgive us.
When our spirits are filled with cynicism and anger,
when the way we live does not bring growth and contains few possibilities for new life,
hear us as we confess.
In our withered living hear us and bring us to life once more.

***

Just as the desert has flowered among us,
God's transforming love is at work,
bringing into bloom the grace that has been planted within you.

***

May each life make large the Spirit of God and may you know the fullness of God's favour resting upon each of you as you leave this place. For see, God is turning the world upside down; the plans of the self-important will come to an end and the way of vulnerability will lead to life.
The Mighty One is doing good things in and through us.
Go and give birth to the justice and love which has been planted within you by the Spirit of God.
Let it be so.

Advent 4

LECTIONARY READINGS

Isaiah 7:10–16
Psalm 80:1–7, 17–19
Romans 1:1–7
Matthew 1:18–25

Giver and receiver of life, hear my thoughts and form my words. Turn my anxieties into comfort and embrace for those I love. O God, you are the closest and most familiar and yet the most unknown. Take this life, narrowed by what is known, and open to me a new way of being. Lead me into the depth and breadth of love. Amen.

***

The season has ripened and the waiting is all but over.
God is with us. God is for us.
Our hearts are often empty, but our hearts yearn to be full.
God is with us. God is for us.
"Yes" can be our prayer.
"Yes" can be our way of life.
God is with us. God is for us. Thanks be to God!

***

You ask for a sign, O people of God,
a sign that God's love is being birthed among you.
I tell you the signs are all around you.
If you know where to look,
you will find them from the depths of the earth to the sky above you.

See, there is a sign:
The hand of the young one reaching out to the old, sharing a word of greeting as they gather this day.
There is another sign:
A songbook held open between partners in life singing of the faith which sustains their union.

And yet another sign:
A sanctuary ready and waiting like a nursery to celebrate the birth of an expected One.

One is coming and this One will be called Emmanuel, God is with us.
So come, see if you can find any more signs of God's love –
among us already and those yet to be revealed –
and may God's love grow in and around us
as we worship Emmanuel this day.

***

God of dreams and dreamers,
you speak to us at all times
and sometimes when we least expect it.
Help us to pay attention to you as did Joseph and Mary
and to be trusting and faithful.
May we continue to see your world
come alive in our world. Amen.

***

One: This Sunday, we light all four of our Advent candles, celebrating the brightness of God's love. Now is the time when we begin to cross the threshold from Advent journeying into Christmas coming.

All: **Come, let us walk in the light of the Lord!** *(Isaiah 2:5)*

Two: *(read while candles are being lit)* In God's promised new heaven and new earth, "the city has no need of sun or moon to shine on it, for the glory of God is its light, and its lamp is the Lamb. The nations will walk by its light, and the rulers of the earth will bring their glory into it." *(Rev. 21:23–24)*

All: **Come, let us walk in the light of the Lord!**

***

Distribute pencils/pens and slips of paper and invite worshippers to seat themselves comfortably. The main purpose is to experience "letting go" in whatever ways God is calling us to release the attachments of our present lives. The leader may play soft meditative music (not Christmas carols). Invite worshippers to write down on pieces of paper the things, people, fears, and whatever else they need to release today, on the brink of Christmas. When complete, have people fold the papers and place them at their own feet.

Close your eyes and take some long deep breaths. Internally scan your body, from the top of your head, your face, to your neck, shoulders, torso, all the way to your toes, and try to consciously release, release, release tension.

Pause. Invite people to reach down and grasp their "attachments" in their hands.

Think about other attachments you might have: attachment to particular ideas of how Christmas "should" go; attachment to an idea of who we are supposed to be, or what will make us happy, or what will make us safe.
Pause.

Now grasp your attachments you've written very tightly. Tighter. Tighter! Now take a deep breath and tighten every muscle in your body. Now release! Let those attachments fall from your hands to the floor. Scan your body for tension and release all of it. God calls us to turn over every attachment; attachment can be a barrier to experiencing and receiving the love and life God has for us.
Pause.

Now, let us receive. Beyond relaxing, open the palms of your hands and let them rest on your knees. If you like, you can even extend your arms over your head. Think about what God might be offering you… what might be a new experience of Christmas?...a new idea about our emerging selves…a deep knowledge that we have enough; enough love, enough life?

Prayer or time of silence.

***

Assured and inspired by God's "yes" to us,
we gladly journey into the unfolding week.
Challenged by the needs of our community and world,
we seek to be a living "yes" to all God's people.
Friends, go in the hope, peace, joy, and love of God.
We go out in the name of Christ and by the power of the Spirit. Amen.

Christmas Eve

LECTIONARY READINGS
Isaiah 9:2–7
Psalm 96
Titus 2:11–14
Luke 2:1–14, (15–20)

The moment is near.
Our feet have brought us close to the place where love is born.
Our hearts are filled with trembling hopes for the future of the world,
hopes that have formed and grown within us
as we have walked this way together.
A star hovers over us and waits in expectation.
Surely the Christ will come and we will find a place for the birthing.

***

Our lives are stilled in trembling hope.
Within a womb of faithfulness,
in ordinary human life,
holiness may be conceived and brought to birth in labour and sighing.
Be still, and hear the promises of God
echoing in the melodies of distant singing.
(moments of silence as Advent candles are lit)

Pause and look, for we may be found among the welcoming –
the ones who greet in joy
the small but true arrival of the Divine in the midst of human life.
Be still, and hear the promises of God
echoing in the melodies of distant singing.

***

O God, we pray that you will create among our lives
a sacred space for the Christ child.
Even as we ask for this,
our lives kneel before you in regret,
as we know the hurt we sometimes cause.

O God, we have not always acted in loving and just ways.
Sometimes we have closed the door to kindness
or turned away people who are different.
Create a space of forgiveness here, we pray.

Sometimes we have been so busy with our own agendas
that we have failed to look for your life lying among us,
the life which invites us to stop and see
a different dream for the world.
Create a space of forgiveness here, we pray.

Then there are moments when we deny ourselves the gifts of vulnerable hope,
bowing to the cynicisms of our day
and refusing to lift our hearts to receive your promises.
Create a space of forgiveness here, we pray.
Come to us in grace, Jesus Christ. Amen.

***

Mercy is unfolding before our eyes.
There is no time nor place where the life of Christ will not create a space for forgiveness.
Let us open the doors of our souls to receive the wonder of this gift:
the holiness of renewed and abundant life.
We are forgiven!
Thanks be to God.

***

After each petition, as the people respond, light a votive candle and create a circle of light around the Advent wreath, or a spiral of light on the Communion table.

One: We pray for all of us who participate in the human story. We pray for all of us who have our being in creation. We light the candles as a symbol of the flame that sustains us. For the leaders of this world, may they be guided by God's will and not their own power.

All: **Light of Christ, love's pure light.**
One: For the citizens of the nations of this earth, may we be guided by equality and common good.
All: **Light of Christ, love's pure light.**
One: For the parents in our lives, may we be guided by humility, responsibility, and patience.
All: **Light of Christ, love's pure light.**
One: For the children in our lives, may we be guided by love, trust, and possibility.
All: **Light of Christ, love's pure light.**
One: For the unsheltered and unprotected, may we be guided by a sense of possibility, and a kindness for strangers.
All: **Light of Christ, love's pure light.**
One: For the innkeepers, workers, and shelter-makers and givers, may we be guided by a sense of gratitude and hospitality.
All: **Light of Christ, love's pure light.**
One: For the shepherds, may we be guided by a calm vigilance and adventurous assurance.
All: **Light of Christ, love's pure light.**
One: For the flora and fauna of creation, may you be guided by a sustainable power and a movement towards redemption.
All: **Light of Christ, love's pure light.**
One: For the messengers of God, may you be guided by wonder and inspiration.
All: **Light of Christ, love's pure light.**
One: For all in whom Christ's love is born today, may we treasure and ponder what we have learned today and may we glorify and praise God for all we hear and see this day, and every day. Amen.
All: **Light of Christ, love's pure light.**

***

O God, Loving Parent of all,
who sent us Jesus Christ to bring hope to the world,
create in us courage to hold your life dear
in all that we are and all that we do.

Inspire us to new heights of life
when we look at the soaring skylines of our cities,
and renew us with the greening of the grass on our hillsides.
Make every singing bird a memory of this day,
and every winding roadway an invitation to walk on
towards your will for us.

SEASON OF CHRISTMAS

Christmas Day

Proper 3 (A, B, C)

LECTIONARY READINGS
Isaiah 52:7–10
Psalm 98
Hebrews 1:1–4, (5–12)
John 1:1–14

Based on Psalm 98

One: O sing to God a new song.
All: God has done marvellous things.
One: O sing to God a new song.
All: for true justice revealed.
One: O sing to God a new song,
All: for steadfast love and faithfulness.
One: O sing to God a new song,
All: let the whole world shout.
One: Make a joyful noise to God, all the earth; break forth into joyous song and sing praises.
Sing: "Joy to the World"

***

Have the four Advent candles already lit.

Christ is born,
and so we light this candle amidst the ones that have illuminated our way through Advent.
This candle reminds us of the light of the world born on this day,
born every day,
in our hearts,
and in the living of Christ's way of love, compassion, and justice.
Light Christ candle.

***

Use the words below to invite people into a time of silent reflection. After a few moments of silence, sing the third verse of "O Little Town of Bethlehem."

Even as the sounds of joy and hope are spread abroad in all the earth,
there will be those who are threatened by this new life.
Even within our own hearts,
there will be moments when we do not, or cannot, hold it dear.
On this day, God calls us to guard love and peace,
to cherish justice and all that is of the life of Christ,
as though that life is a precious gift.
On this day, God calls us to guard and cherish all that is in our own life here,
which waits to be born and to grow in grace among us.

***

You are the new song.
You are the next beat in my heart.
You are praise and possibility.
You are the present and the future.
I believe the Light of the World has come on this day.
I see it now in all days.
Those gone and those to come are aflame in love.
Your love wrapped in human form,
Your love learned in justice and mercy,
Your love risen over death.
I believe love has come on this day.
I believe love has and will always come.

***

O God, you have placed in our hands
the greatest gift of all – your own holy life.
Even as we sing with joy today, we know that this is a grave responsibility.
We pray that we may have the wisdom and faithfulness to cherish this life,

both within this community and in the world.
We pray for the ones who care
for the vulnerable life of love in our day;
those who protect it with costly loyalty.
We long for you, O Christ,
waiting in hope for justice and freedom.
(Offer specific prayers for justice.)

We realize that there are life experiences of loss and betrayal
which make it hard to enter into the celebrations
of family and friends on this day.
We embrace with love and care
all for whom Christmas is a painful time.
(Offer specific prayers of compassion.)

Come into all the world with your hope, Jesus Christ,
and claim the earth again as the birthplace for your promise.
This we pray in faith.
Amen.

***

Let us leave this place with lifted hearts.
And may our lives live out your promise, O God.
May your peace and love become real in all that we do, Jesus Christ.
And may the Holy Spirit dance in celebration ahead of us.
Amen.

First Sunday after Christmas Day

LECTIONARY READINGS

Isaiah 63:7–9
Psalm 148
Hebrews 2:10–18
Matthew 2:13–23

God of old ways and new starts, give us the courage and wisdom to honour both. May our ears hear and eyes see the ways that every part of your created world shouts, "Hallelujah." Help us know, love, and live the Christmas born in each of us today! Hallelujah! Amen.

***

Slowly process a candle down the aisle while a variety of female voices read the lines below.

angels unfurl their wings
roadways straighten
stars slide
brokenness heals
time hesitates
creation bows
promise whispers
blind folk see
darkness fades
deserts bloom
captives walk out
valleys fill
flesh stretches
yokes are broken
prisoners go free
and straw makes a bed for a saviour for those who hold their breath

***

Almighty God, daily you bless us with the gift of living in your universe, breathing air, and being awake. On this first Sunday in our new

Christmas reality, we share the divine life of Jesus the Christ who came to share our humanity and who now lives and reigns with you and the Holy Spirit, one God, now and forever. Amen.

***

Light the four Advent candles and the white Christ candle prior to the spoken prayer.

Both energized and wearied by days just past,
we gather in your re-creative love, O God,
to rest and re-focus.

Open our lives to amazement.
Open our imaginations to possibility.
Open our souls to healing presence;
you in us, and we in each other.
Amen.

***

Allow a generous amount of silence before this prayer, inviting people to be conscious of their breathing; inhaling the abundance of God's ever-renewing spirit and exhaling what is stale, lifeless, and in need of renewal. Set the people going on this then step back and wait for the appropriate moment to begin the spoken prayer. Invite one-word responses at the end of the prayer.

Friends, let us pray.

Creator of all things, intricate and sublime,
mover of distant planets and stars,
spirit of busy subatomic particles.

Every aspect of your world drums out a reassuring message
of goodness and love being close at hand –
from the returning and retreating of great seas
to a tiny birdsong that enflames
even the dullest of mornings.

What is it that prevents us from seeing?
How is it that we don't take it all in?
Why is it that we cannot rest and treasure?

Hear our confessions;
those stale and empty things that keep us back and keep us bound…
(one-word responses, spoken or silent)

***

Held and encouraged by God,
we offer our confessions
as a body exhales spent and tired breath.
The peace of Christ fills us as we draw into our depths
the promise of wholeness and gift of renewed joy.
Amen.

***

Living God,
you came among us to share our whole lives:
Our joys and our laughter,
our fears and our dangers.
You go with us in times of trials and suffering.
You call us to come into safety.
Encourage us to trust that your love is wrapped around us
even when we feel most frightened,
most alone, most lost.
Help us to comfort and be comforted,
to welcome and be welcomed,
to shelter and be sheltered.

As you have provided hospitality to us
may we offer it to others
and receive it with grace,
and so enable all people to feel safe
and at home wherever they are. Amen.

***

Where are we going?
We go to befriend the lonely.
Where are we going?
We go to heal the sick.
Where are we going?
We go to feed the hungry.
Let us go, then, to be God's presence in our world, to journey with those who need to know that they are not alone. And know that God – companion of the sojourner, friend of the sinner, and comforter of the lost – will be with you wherever you go. Amen.

***

SEASON AFTER THE EPIPHANY

Epiphany of the Lord

LECTIONARY READINGS
Isaiah 60:1–6
Psalm 72:1–7, 10–14
Ephesians 3:1–12
Matthew 2:1–12

We thank you, O God, for revealing your love in the gift of a child. Stir our hopes. Prepare us for mysteries that can change us. Ready us for dreams that may send us in a new direction. Ground us in our wisdom, and help us follow your call.

***

God of all life, we come to worship.
May we see through the wrapping paper,
the festive trees, and the glass ornaments,
to see the Christ child among us, born as one of us.
Help us discover the child in all the epiphany moments
of our living and worshipping here.
Then send us out to reveal your presence
and your promise to this world. Amen.

***

God of grace,
in this moment and all through this day
may we know the warmth of welcome,
may we feel love surrounding us. Amen.

***

The prayer leader may journey around the worship space leading prayers from different parts of the space.

Journeying God,
beyond the hills lies a new journey
into the places of conflict.
Hear us as we pray for these places.
(Pause here for silence or for the prayer leader to name areas of concern for conflict.)
May we find the child here
and may these places be shaped
by the peace that shaped Jesus' living.

Journeying God,
beyond the hills lies a new journey
into the places of hunger.
Hear us as we pray for these places.
(Pause here for silence or for the prayer leader to name areas of concern for hunger.)
May the child be found here
and may these places be shaped
by the hunger for justice that shaped Jesus' living.

Journeying God,
beyond the hills lies a new journey
into the places of shadows.
Hear us as we pray for these places.
(Pause here for silence or for the prayer leader to name areas of concern for illness or doubt or grief.)
May this be a place to find the child,
and may these places be shaped by the truth that shaped Jesus' living.

***

We have beheld a wonder –
human-shaped and light-filled –
a wonder that holds all potential,
making worthwhile our journeys
to seek out the Christ child again in every unstable place.

We have beheld a wonder –
God-shaped and human-filled –
for a world longing for light.
And so we travel on into an unknown future
yet filled with the possibility of birth.
We wonder about every epiphany
waiting to reveal the hand of God,
in some unexpected time and place.

We have beheld a wonder –
love-shaped and love-filled –
a sacrifice for God to let go the son into this world.
And so we turn from here to a new direction,
and we leave the child to find the saviour
already changing the universe with grace
towards love and calling us home.

***

Guiding God, your light beams into our lives, offering us what we cannot do without: hope. Help us hear your hope, and draw nearer to you and your truth as we encounter your word together today. In Jesus' name we pray. Amen.

***

God, your power and love are ancient, yet ever new.
Launch us into your world to see afresh the love born into the world at each moment.
May it be so. Amen.

First Sunday after the Epiphany

LECTIONARY READINGS

Isaiah 42:1–9
Psalm 29
Acts 10:34–43
Matthew 3:13–17

Mighty God, fill us with the blessings of new life in you. Open our hearts and minds to receive your bountiful Spirit as our companion, directing our steps as we move into the world as witnesses to Christ's power and love. Amen.

***

Inspired by Isaiah 42:1–9
Pour water into the baptismal font after these sentences.

Through the prophet's voice,
words from the Creator of All are perceived:
"Here are my servants,
whom my Spirit strengthens and encourages.
In you my soul delights and my Spirit is with you."
Held in the loving grasp of the Spirit,
a fire burns in the heart of this community,
illuminating outward in ever-expanding circles of justice.
May you be empowered by the Spirit
to do a new thing with God.

***

Pour water into the baptismal font after this call to worship if you have not already done so.

We are called to this place to find a new way:
a way of grace, hope, faith, life.
God calls and we come.
Come, and let go of that which is worn out:
worn out habits,

worn out dogmas
worn out resentments,
worn out burdens.
God calls and we come.
This time is blessed and made sacred by Spirit who heals us,
reconnects us,
redirects us,
empowers us.
God blesses and we praise.
Come, and receive blessing, freedom, forgiveness, love.
God blesses and we praise.

***

Created by God and baptized into Christ's Spirit,
a voice deep down and all around
assures us that we are beloved of God.
Yet we can be quick to forget our true nature.
Comfortable with what is familiar and easy,
we quench the fire within our hearts.
Defined by our past and fearful of the future
we make excuses for our lack of responsiveness.
We confess silently now that which keeps us from knowing fully and living courageously
our beloved-ness in God.
(moments of silence)

***

Perform the noted motions as you offer these words of assurance. People may feel free to mimic your motions, but refrain from interrupting the flow of the service with an invitation or instructions for them to do the motions.

We are beloved of God as declared in the act of baptism *(cup hands in front of body and make a dipping motion with your hands).*

The Spirit of God is upon us, giving shape to our life and loving *(rest the palms of your hands on your head).*

Great and abundant love flows over every part of our being *(trace fingertips down the sides of your head and body).*

Thanks be to God.

***

For this renewal of baptism in smaller congregations, place bowls of water around the space and invite people to gather round in small groups. For larger congregations, stand near the baptismal font.

God calls us to the water to find a new way:
a new grace,
a new hope,
a new faith,
a new life.
God calls, we come.
Come to the water and let go of the worn out:
worn out habits,
worn out pains,
worn out angers,
worn out burdens.
God calls, we come.
God blesses the water and it
heals us,
cleans us,
renews us,
refreshes us.
God blesses; we praise.
Come to the water and receive
blessing,
freedom,
mercy,
love.
God blesses; we praise.

(Hold up one of the bowls of water or place hands in the font.)

Gracious God, your spirit moved over the waters of chaos to bring forth cosmos. Your spirit moves in the waters of the womb to bring forth life. Your spirit rains and pours and floods in rivers and oceans and veins; cleansing, purifying, anointing all creation for your service. Bless this water with your presence. Amen.

Invite people forward for the renewal of baptism. Place your hands in the water and then draw a cross on each person's forehead as you say these words:

God has created you and named you Beloved. Live for God.

***

O God, we look at our feet and see the unfolding possibilities.
May we move in directions of service.
We look at our hands and see a future of compassion.
May we seek to do the work of justice.
We look into our hearts and see love and the connection.
May we be shaped into beloved community.

***

The anointing of baptism is fresh upon us and the Spirit's voice rings in our ears:
You are my beloved community and I am pleased with you.
Let us go in the assurance of God's love and travel courageously
into the unfolding possibilities within and around us.

Second Sunday after the Epiphany

LECTIONARY READINGS

Isaiah 49:1–7
Psalm 40:1–11
1 Corinthians 1:1–9
John 1:29–42

Loving God, thank you for pouring out your bountiful Spirit on all your children. Empower us to rejoice in the changes that come when we meet Jesus. Amen.

***

O God,
when we least expect you, you appear.
You appear in the faces of strangers and friends,
you appear in places of danger and calm,
you appear in our times of weakness and strength.
Open our eyes to see you here and now
and then open our mouths to speak and sing and shout
the good news that you are here, you are there, you are everywhere.
Amen.

***

One: Jesus invited the disciples to come and see.
All: **Jesus invites us to come and see.**
Two: Jesus invited the disciples to notice God's presence.
All: **Jesus invites us to notice God's presence.**
Three: Jesus invited the disciples to follow.
All: **Jesus invites us to follow.**
One: Come, friends, let us notice what is here among us.
Two: Let us notice God is present here.
Three: Let us follow God's call *(pause)* to be here.
If feasible with your worshipping community and space, invite people to come forward, or to form a circle around the edge of the worship area. Otherwise, people may remain in their seats.

One: God asks us to remember that God is present in each of us,
Two: to remember that God is present in me, in you, in this community.
Three: Sometimes we forget. We may see, but we do not know God.
All: **"I saw," John said, "but I myself did not know him."**
One: With all of our being, we need to look more closely.
Two: We need to look more clearly.
Three: We need to look more carefully.
One: We need to say to each other,
"When I do not recognize God in you, remind me to look more deeply."
Let us turn to those near us and say,
"When I do not recognize God in you, remind me to look more deeply."

If you are standing in a circle, the leaders can begin the phrase from different parts of the circle. In this way, in a rather confused jumble of words and sounds, many voices are speaking at once. When the phrase has gone around the circle, or when everyone in the pews has had sufficient time to speak and hear the phrase a few times, continue.

One: Jesus invited the disciples to follow.
All: **Jesus invites us to follow.**
One: Jesus invited the disciples to notice God's presence.
Two: Jesus invites us to notice God's presence.
Three: Jesus invited the disciples to come and see.
All: **Jesus invites us to come and see.**
One: We have come together to behold.
Two: Now go forth into the world to behold
Three: more closely, more clearly, more carefully.
All: **Amen.**

***

Place twelve candles of different shapes and heights on a table covered in green cloth. Light three of them after each stanza.

God of incandescent, healing light;
light that glows even in the deepest shadows,
be a flame in our hearts at this time of prayer.

As we bring to mind the needs of our world
and your call to be a presence wherever we may journey,
in and through us
let there be light and love for all
(moment of reflection as three candles are lit).

When we are locked in deep prisons of religious hatreds,
cultural loathing, and bigotry,
in and through us,
let there be light and love for all
(moment of reflection as three candles are lit).

When we are held captive to fear and anxiety,
or when we feel the dread of despair,
or the grey void of futility,
in and through us
let there be light and love for all
(moment of reflection as three candles are lit).

When we are numbed by loss or suffering
or when we have dashed hopes for justice and peace in our time,
in and through us
let there be light and love for all
(moment of reflection as three candles are lit).

Giver of courage,
gift us with renewed faith,
and fill us with an unyielding hope.
In and through us
let there be light and love for all.
Amen.

***

Beloved of God!
We are here.
You who have been known in love before your birth
and called for love since the day of your birth,

go into the world
as warm and healing waves of light.
Go in the spirit of peace
with simplicity
and clothed in the compassion of Christ.
Amen.

Third Sunday after the Epiphany

LECTIONARY READINGS
Isaiah 9:1–4
Psalm 27:1, 4–9
1 Corinthians 1:10–18
Matthew 4:12–23

Turn our hearts to you, O God, and open us to the gradual unfolding of your call in our lives. Bind us together as one Body of Christ, and be our hope as we seek to live into your mission of love. Amen.

***

Hear the waters of baptism calling
and inviting us to be renewed
by this sign of God's love.
We answer the call to be God's people
and we live in the ways of the Christ.

Hear the Spirit of God among us
reminding us that we are
beloved children of God.
We answer the call to be God's people
and we live in the ways of the Christ.

Hear the Spirit of Christ calling,
"Come and see where I am alive
within this community and beyond."
We answer the call to be God's people
and we live in the ways of the Christ.

Hear the invitation of God
to leave behind ways grown old
and follow in new paths of service.
We answer the call to be God's people
and we live in the ways of the Christ.

***

Holy One,
speak to our lives this day.
Order our paths.
Call us again to follow the light and the stronghold of our lives. Amen.

***

Invite the people to meditate as they reflect on the following.

Holy One:
We rush to and fro…but do we seek your face? *(Pause.)*
We wait…but do we wait for your word to speak to our lives? *(Pause.)*
We ask and inquire…but do we pursue your presence? *(Pause.)*
We make sacrifices…but do we make them to praise you? *(Pause.)*
We sing…but do we sing with joy? *(Pause.)*

Most of the time, we rush to and fro in confusion and in fear, without aim or direction, responding to the most immediate demand for our attention. We worry that there is not enough time in our day, or space in our lives for one more "to do" from God. We close our ears to God's call on our lives. We fear that turning to God could be the time drain that sinks our schedules and brings our lives to a tipping point.

Gracious God, forgive our preoccupation and our lives ordered by panic and pressure from co-workers, acquaintances, friends, and calendars. Call us again to seek your face and follow the Christ. As we turn to you, help us see this tipping point as an opportunity to see the whole world and our lives in a new light. Amen.

***

One: Jesus said: Follow me and live in the ways of God.
Two: To you who feel secure in faith,
and you who have doubts and skepticisms, Jesus says,
One: follow me.
Two: To you who have been faithful in your commitments
and you who have failed or been failed, Jesus says,
One: follow me.

Two: This is a time for new starts and renewed starts;
a time to follow more deeply the loving ways of God.

***

O God of the universe,
Christ of incarnated wisdom,
Spirit of the green-blue earth,
you illumine us with your great light of love
and, in this time, we pledge our love to you.
May we be strong in our resolve
and may our bodies be filled with your passion
as we commit ourselves to being your healing love in this world.

***

One: Repent, turn back to God,
so that the way of God can be made real within you.
Two: As we turn and follow the vision of God before us,
we experience the liberating joy of living in God's way.
Thanks be to God. Amen.

***

We have received the light of God in the words of scripture,
in the faithful witness of our sisters and brothers,
in the bread and wine of the table,
in the music of our voices.
Go now and share this light in words of peace,
in witness of love,
in the sharing of wealth,
in the joy of good news.
Amen.

Fourth Sunday after the Epiphany

LECTIONARY READINGS

Micah 6:1–8
Psalm 15
1 Corinthians 1:18–31
Matthew 5:1–12

O God, you turn things upside down, calling the wise to embrace your folly. Help us to grow in acknowledging our need for you. Open us to the vision of your reign on earth, and strengthen us to do our part. Amen.

***

Based on Micah 6:8

One: God has told you, what is good, and what God requires.
All: **What is *good?* What *does* God require of us?**
One: To do justice
All: **with God**
One: and to love kindness
All: **with God**
One: and to walk humbly
All: **with God.**
One: Come let us worship God.

***

Pull on our hearts this day, O God.
Unbind our lives from the conventions of this world, we pray.
Amen.

***

Give a brief introduction to this prayer in order for the beginning to make sense. It seeks to highlight how conventional wisdom is not the way of Christ. Explain that you will cue the people to begin each stanza by ringing a bell.

(Ring bell.)
We have heard it said:
It's really just common sense.
Self-protection at all costs.
Conquer or be conquered.
Charity always begins at home;
and we often believe without thinking
(observe silence followed by bell).

We have heard it said:
Of course our culture is superior.
Warheads make for peace and security.
Wealth will buy happiness.
Celebrities are role models;
and we often believe without thinking
(observe silence followed by bell).

We have heard it said:
Nothing can be done to change that.
The poor will always be with us.
I am not my brother or sister's keeper.
Tears are for women and children;
and we often believe without thinking
(observe silence followed by bell).

God of surprises and non-convention,
grace us with a vulnerability and openness
to hear the wise and lyrical voice of Jesus anew.
May our ways of seeing, acting, and responding
be changed in light of Jesus' great love of you
and the world of your making.
Amen.

***

One: For the poor in spirit, those who mourn, the meek,
those who hunger and thirst for righteousness, the merciful,
the pure in heart, and the peacemakers

All: **we pray: May God's will be done.**
One: For the rich and powerful to see God's reality and love as a path to liberation
All: **we pray: May God's will be done.**
One: For those who have given up hope
that liberation, change and transformation are possible
All: **we pray: May God's will be done.**

***

Friends of God,
followers of Jesus
and people of Spirit,
go into this day and week alive to the vision
that is God's realm of peace, joy, and compassion.
We will hold true to our call.
We will continually seek the grace and wisdom of Jesus the Christ.
Amen.

***

Holy God, as we abide in your presence, help us know your saving acts. Strengthen us to do what is good in your eyes. Guide us as we walk humbly with you, and shape our lives to love kindness. Teach us and provoke us to acts of justice. Amen.

Fifth Sunday after the Epiphany

LECTIONARY READINGS

Isaiah 58:1–9a, (9b–12)
Psalm 112:1–9, (10)
1 Corinthians 2:1–12, (13–16)
Matthew 5:13–20

Enlivening God, you call us to be salt, adding flavour to the world. You call us to be light, illuminating and restoring beauty. Give us courage to respond, so that your presence may be revealed through all the world. Amen.

***

Gracious God, grant us eyes to see your vision for your people. Help us rise as a light, as we delight in your commands. Amen.

***

Our hearts lie open before you,
God of love, God of mercy:
All that we are, all that you call us to be.

Our deepest yearnings rise before you,
God of wonderment, God of soul:
All that we are, all that you call us to be.

Our adoration is reserved for you alone,
God of beauty, God of grace:
All that we are, all that you call us to be.
(moments of silence)

Through this time of worship, renew within us the vision of your beauty,
restoring our own gift of radiance:
All that we are, all that you call us to be.

In the name of Christ, through the love of the Spirit.
Amen.

***

Based on Isaiah 58:11–12

One: Light of the world,
you guide us in your ways
and satisfy our needs.
We offer our prayers for ourselves and others.

(Pause for people to name their needs and the needs of the community, aloud or in the silence.)

In your mercy,
All: **hear our prayers.**
One: Water us like a garden
that we may grow to serve you.
Strengthen us,
and fill us with a resolve that never fails.
Rebuild, repair, and restore our community. Amen.

***

One: In silence, we contemplate the injustices that exist in the community.
(Provide a time of silence.) Our Redeemer,
All: **forgive us.**
One: In silence, we lament the ways our community has fallen short of shining a light on God's glory.
(Provide a time of silence.) Our Redeemer,
All: **forgive us.**
One: For times when we have let busyness of life dominate and oppress,
All: **forgive us.**
One: For times when we have turned away from the needs and troubles of others,
All: **forgive us.**
One: Guide us as we practice righteousness and deal generously as we conduct our affairs.
All: **Amen.**

Sixth Sunday after the Epiphany

Proper 1. If this is the Sunday before Ash Wednesday, this Proper may be replaced, in those churches using Transfiguration readings on this day, by the readings for the Last Sunday after the Epiphany.

LECTIONARY READINGS
Deuteronomy 30:15–20 *or* Sirach 15:15–20
Psalm 119:1–8
1 Corinthians 3:1–9
Matthew 5:21–37

Life-giving God, in Jesus you show us a new way. When we are tempted to jealousy and anger, teach us to respond in love. Unfold to us the heart of your gospel, and strengthen us to work together to bring about your realm on earth. Amen.

***

Explorer of our hearts, discerner of our souls, we invite you into the depths of our struggles. We open the locked doors. With words of love and the boldness of truth, we ask you to knock on the hardest places in our hearts and to soften them so that we may love you and love our neighbours. Amen.

***

God of our deepest yearnings,
give us devoted hearts that seek
to listen, think, and feel anew.
Open in us the wisdom of Jesus,
with the courage needed
to travel his life-giving road.
Amen.

***

God of love and life, hear our prayer
for renewed ways of heart and mind.
For we seek a faith
bold in its authenticity,
generous in its practice,
and always deepening at its heart.
O God, hear our prayer.

God of love and life, hear our prayer
for a renewal of hope and action.
For we seek a faith
that longs for shared futures,
is reconciling in its expression,
and always deepening in its heart.
O God, hear our prayer.

God of love and life, hear our prayer
for a renewing of trust and compassion.
For we seek a faith
willing to co-suffer and heal,
tenacious in its desire for justice,
and always deepening in its heart.
O God, hear our prayer.

***

May your yes be a yes! May your no be a no! May your words come straight from your heart so that when you speak them God's love is felt for miles, and truth becomes the most cooperative act. Amen.

***

As people of heart and spirit,
go boldly into the new week,
fully expecting opportunities for greater love
to be placed squarely in your path.
Pray often.
Speak wisely.

Act justly.
Breathe and feel deeply.

May the wisdom of Christ,
the yearnings of God,
and the friendship of the Spirit,
inspire and uphold you,
this day and always.
Amen.

Seventh Sunday after the Epiphany

Proper 2. If this is the Sunday before Ash Wednesday, this Proper may be replaced, in those churches using Transfiguration readings on this day, by the readings for the Last Sunday after the Epiphany.

LECTIONARY READINGS
Leviticus 19:1–2, 9–18
Psalm 119:33–40
1 Corinthians 3:10–11, 16–23
Matthew 5:38–48

Holy Love, comfort us with the love that challenges our hearts. Steadfast Strength, firm up our foundations in the reassurance of the grace of Jesus Christ. Perfect Love, make perfect our understanding of the love that perfects us. Amen.

***

Teach us, O God, the way of your commandments and give us grace to follow where you lead. You break down the walls that separate us from one another. In everyone we meet, help us to see a neighbour and reach out in love and service. Amen.

***

God, whose spirit dwells within us,
fill our space with your love
that we may be holy and perfect in its presence. Amen.

***

Based on Psalm 119:33–40
Teach us, O God, the ways of your will
and we will follow it to the end.
Give us understanding,
that we may honour your law of love
and treasure it deep within our hearts.
(silent reflection)

Lead us in the paths of your desire,
for we delight in them.
Bend our hearts to your teaching,
and not to selfish gain.
(silent reflection)

Close our eyes to empty, material things,
but through your words of wisdom
give us renewed life.
Keep your promise of love
so that all may be enfolded in it.
(silent reflection)

Save us from words of hatred and violence,
for your ways are just and good.
See how we yearn for your wisdom;
through your healing presence
you give us life.
(silent reflection)

***

Welcomed here by the Spirit,
We are held by God's love,
made whole in the kindness of Christ,
and set free to be a people
of mercy and compassion for others.
God's peace is our peace to know and share.

***

Beyond our knowing,
and well beyond our seeing, O God,
your word of healing grace
extends to the whole cosmos;
to every creature,
every fibre of existence and being.
What we consider to be beyond redemption,

or those whom we think are somehow outside your reach,
are the very ones you call us to love and befriend.

We pray, then, for the most difficult of all,
our enemies;
Perceived or real, in far-away lands or close by.
Those that have betrayed our trust,
misrepresented our character,
or injured us in any way.
May we have the heart of Wisdom.
May we be filled with the gift of mercy
and be set free to love anew.
(silent reflection)

We pray for when we are seemingly beyond the care
and reach of "civilized" societies:
When we are impoverished by the great wealth of others,
when we seek new and hopeful lands,
and when we are lost in a mind of our own,
suffering the alienation and confusion
of mental illness or depression.
May we have the heart of Wisdom,
may we be filled with the gift of mercy
and be set free to love anew.
(silent reflection)

Finally, we pray for this community of faith
and all communities of good will.
Together may we live out the dynamic vision
of expanding boundaries of humanity,
gathering and including in the creative love of God
those we loath, those we fear,
those held at arm's-length;
all those, including ourselves,
in need of an accepting and peaceable embrace.
May we have the heart of Wisdom,
may we be filled with the gift of mercy
and be set free to love anew.
(silent reflection)

In the name of the One who came to re-gather and save, Jesus, the Christ.
Amen.

***

As the universe continues to expand,
and as the mighty rivers run wider to cover the sea,
go out into the world of God's making
as bearers of a love that knows no boundaries;
mindful of how demanding this call can be,
yet alive to its vision of enfolding goodness and beauty.
And so may the wisdom of Christ,
the compassion of God,
and the friendship of the Spirit
bear you up
and fill you with renewed strength
for life's journey.

Eighth Sunday after the Epiphany

Proper 3. If this is the Sunday before Ash Wednesday, this Proper may be replaced, in those churches using Transfiguration readings on this day, by the readings for the Last Sunday after the Epiphany.

LECTIONARY READINGS
Isaiah 49:8–16a
Psalm 131
1 Corinthians 4:1–5
Matthew 6:24–34

Bountiful and generous God, increase our joy in the unlimited riches you provide. When worry and anxiety overwhelm our hearts, enliven us with your Spirit to trust in your ways, which always put love first. In Christ. Amen.

***

Like an infant quieted at its mother's breast,
like a child holding the hand of a trusted grandparent,
we are calm and quiet in Love's presence.

Like a farmer at the end of a fruitful day,
like a kitten purring over a bowl of milk,
we are calm and quiet in Love's presence.

Like a community of faith gathered for worship,
like the smell of a candle lit and burning,
we are calm and quiet in Love's presence.

***

Breathe deeply the Spirit of Love within and among us.
(Take a breath in through your nose and release it through your mouth. Mimic the slowly expanding chest with your hands.)

Breathe deeply the loving air of trust that surrounds us.
(Repeat the breathing actions.)

Breathe deeply…
(Repeat the breathing actions.)

Breathe deeply and receive forgiveness.
(Repeat the breathing actions.)

Breathe deeply
(breathe in)
and, as air flows from your body,
(breathe out)
God's love flows in your words and actions,
filling the world with goodness.

***

Merciful Creator, we breathe in your Spirit
and fill our nostrils
with the smells of your creation.
We fill our eyes and ears
with the sights and sounds of your beauty.
We give thanks for the gift of our Earth home
and are mindful of the destruction
our lack of connection has caused.
Hear our prayers.
(time of silence)

God of community and care,
we touch the tenderness
of those with whom we share life.
We give thanks with our breath,
our senses, our singing, and our silence,
for the gifts of loving relationships.
Secure in this love, we bring our fears,
our worries, our anxieties about those we love
and those with whom we interact on a daily basis.
Hear our prayers.
(time of silence)

God of joy and abundance,
we wake up in the night worried
about our health, our finances, our children,
and ailing friends and family members.
But we are also deeply concerned for those whose stories are known
through the words of others
and for whom justice is a far flung hope.
Hear our prayers.

***

We have been illumined by the extraordinary and wise teachings of the Christ. Now live as the Christ ones; at home, at work, at school, at play, wherever your days take you. Seek the way of right-ness, put love first, and may Love's presence surround you on all sides. **Amen.**

Last Sunday after the Epiphany

Transfiguration Sunday

LECTIONARY READINGS
Exodus 24:12–18
Psalm 2 *or* Psalm 99
2 Peter 1:16–21
Matthew 17:1–9

O Mystery, O Holy Love, may our hearts be stilled. May our souls be porous to absorb your divine grace. May we hear, feel, and understand the words that quench our burning desire: "My Beloved with whom I am well pleased." Amen.

***

One: We have come into the presence of God
and captured Isaiah's vision of peace
where the wolf lives with the lamb
and the leopard lies down with the calf.
Two: God is in this holy place.
All: **We come to worship in peace.**

One: We have sat with Jesus on the mountain
and we immersed ourselves
in the extraordinary and wise teachings of Jesus;
the challenging way of love for all.
Two: God is calling again.
All: **We come to worship in love.**

One: We travel with Jesus and disciples of long ago,
and in the glory of the clouds
hear God's affirmation of the One
whose life dazzled with the reign of God.
Two: God is calling again.
All: **We come to worship in joy.**

***

We may not be able to climb a hill for you, O God,
but we gather to worship you in this place.
We may never see you transfigured in glory in our presence,
but we witness to your transforming power in our living.
We may not have the words to explain all that you are,
but we have hearts that want to worship all that you are.
Enable us to meet you in your glory around us,
that we may worship you in truth and love.

***

God's Spirit affirms: You are my Beloved; with you I am well pleased.
Love never forgets and is quick to forgive.
We can trust the Spirit's affirmation
and live with confidence
that we are the Beloved of God,
forgiven and free.

***

Invite people to begin with a breath. Ask them to inhale for five counts, to hold their breath for five counts, and to exhale for five counts. Lead them in this breathing for three breaths to give an oxygen boost to the brain, creating an experience of spaciousness in the body and a feeling of concentration in the mind.

God of Glory, devouring fire, we seek to attend to your mystery.
With each breath, we enter the cloud and find ourselves not cast in shadow, but bathed in love.
We pray for us who are caught in fear, that we may be absorbed in wonder.
We pray for us who are distracted by menial messages, that we may attend to prophetic ones.
We pray for us who are stuck by our own interpretations and versions of truth, that we may be moved by the Holy Spirit.

We pray that we may be bold enough to get up when Jesus calls us and to pray as Jesus teaches:
(your version of the prayer that Jesus taught).

***

God's love surrounds you.
May you meet the transforming power of God,
may you hear the voice of God calling you into the world,
and may you know yourself to be beloved in the Christ.
Amen.

SEASON OF LENT

Lent 1

LECTIONARY READINGS

Genesis 2:15–17; 3:1–7
Psalm 32
Romans 5:12–19
Matthew 4:1–11

God of the journey, you meet us in the wilderness places of our lives, where we are stretched and tested. Walk with us and hold us on the pathway. Grant us wisdom and flexibility that we may grow in grace and love. Amen.

***

Based on Joel 2:1–2, 12–17
(Play some solemn trumpet music or a recording of thunder and heavy rain. As the leader begins, let the music fade.)

Like the sound of a trumpet or the crack of thunder,
God calls us to return.
Return from where? *(Pause.)*
Where have we been? *(Pause.)*
Where *have* we been? *(Pause.)*
Sometimes in the busyness of life,
it's hard to stop and remember what we're doing.
Let's take a moment
to think back over the past week…
or month…or year.
Let us consider what we have done with our time,
how we have used our abilities,
how we have spent our money,
what we have done with our energy.
Where has our heart been?

(A moment for silence with only the sound of the trumpet or the thunderstorm being heard.)
Like the sound of a trumpet or the crack of thunder,
God calls us to return.
God invites us to come home
from wherever we have let ourselves wander.
Sometimes we have strayed only a little.
Sometimes we have lost our way.
No matter.
From wherever we are in our lives,
God calls us to return,
to come home to God
who is gracious and merciful,
slow to anger,
abounding in steadfast love.
Come, let us return to our God.

***

Friends of God, welcome.
May the Spirit of Christ be with you.
And also with you.

As we begin the Season of Lent
make yourself at home
in the unfolding
presence of Love
that nestles,
nourishes,
and gives renewed strength
for the journey of faith.
Amen.

***

God of love and mercy,
we gather today from different places –
both of location and life experience.

Some of us arrive content,
others muddled and fractured,
still others somewhere in between.

God of love and mercy,
at the beginning of the Lenten season,
we pray for a willingness to be held
in all that we are.
We come daring to believe
that in your embrace
joy and hope arises anew.

***

Invite those gathered to imagine being held by Love. They might create a cup with their hands or fold their arms across their chests like a hug in order to help with this imagining.

Grateful for forgiveness, O God,
and amazed by your warmth of heart,
we would be opened,
giving words to difficult feelings,
seeking healing for old, yet tender, wounds.
Hold us;
in your love may we rest and be renewed *(pause).*

For the times we have
deceived ourselves and others
with divided thoughts and purposes,
creating emptiness of soul
and unhappy relationships.
Hold us;
in your love may we rest and be renewed *(pause).*

And for the times we remain silent,
fearful of inner truths,
resistant to real change
and truthful, intimate exchange.

Hold us;
in your love may we rest and be renewed *(pause).*

***

Creating God,
the universe is a vast and awesome place;
our world is full of wonder, and beauty can be found
in fertile valleys and desert spaces.
Thank you for the ever-changing cloud formations
and the constant ebb and flow of the sea.
We praise you for plant life: for rainforests and bush;
for the flower that grows through the concrete path.
Thank you for the abundance of animal life:
for birds that fly free and pets that keep us company.
Thank you for the people who nurture and support us
and give meaning to our lives.
We reflect on the story of our human journey:
Unlike the Garden of Eden described in scripture,
we do not live together in harmony;
the natural world is constantly changing
and we are concerned about encroaching desert,
urban wilderness, and environmental choices that bring destruction.

We have inherited a humanity that knows hunger,
broken relationships, and death.
We own our share in the making of wrong decisions and their consequences;
we acknowledge and lament our part
in contributing to suffering in the world, unintentionally as well as consciously.
Today we are led by the Spirit with Jesus into the wilderness.
Help us to find a path through the desert places, to fullness of life for all.

***

This prayer is read by two voices, one male and one female.

Both: While I kept silence,
my body wasted away
through my groaning all day long.
One: While we keep silence
those who need bread are left hungry.
Two: We confess the times
we have not spoken up for the hungry
and our silence has left hunger as our witness.
(silence)

One: While we keep silence,
those who need a sign are left alone.
Two: We confess the times we
have waited for divine intervention
rather than reaching out in love to one another
and our silence has left loneliness as our witness.
(silence)

One: While we keep silence,
those who need peace shout into the distance.
Two: We confess the times we have silently
gone along with the world
rather than pursuing your demands for justice,
and our silence has left distrust as our witness.
(silence)

One: While we keep silence,
those who need comfort
receive no comforting word.
Two: We confess those times we have been tempted to stand back
rather than crossing the gulf
to enter relationship with one another
and our silence has left despair as our witness.
(silence)

***

Repeat these words of pardon three times, with **One** *saying them first, then* ***Two****, then both voices saying them together.*

Fill our mouths with words of peace,
our hearts with longing for justice,
and our lives with acts of love,
that we may be tempted to trust you
and live for you each day.

Lent 2

LECTIONARY READINGS

Genesis 12:1–4a
Psalm 121
Romans 4:1–5, 13–17
John 3:1–17 *or* Matthew 17:1–9

Wind of God, blow through us and refresh us. Blow through us and help us. Blow through us and bring us new life. Blow away the things that prevent us from seeing your life in the whole of creation, and show us ways to help the healing of your world. Amen.

***

This responsive phrase is one that can be used throughout the service at different times and moments, such as before scripture readings or before the sermon.

When we ask our questions
you hear us.
When we speak to you
you listen to us.
When we seek you out
you show yourself to us.
When we do not understand
you tell us again.

***

God, may your mystery surround us
and your light shine on us.
May your Spirit explore with us
and be our companion.
May what we do not understand
send us on a journey with you today.
Amen.

***

This guided meditation imagines us sitting by Jesus as Nicodemus did. Place two chairs facing each other and invite people to imagine sitting in one chair with Jesus in the other. If possible, dim the lights.

Jesus, here I sit by you. The night settles around us
and I find myself shaping many questions
about my life and my times and my living in this world.
You say I cannot enter your realm
without being born anew.
Yet I confess the ways I cling
to the habits and the patterns
that keep me from living and sharing my life to the full.
Hear me, my Saviour, hear me. *(silence)*

I hear your words: "What is born of flesh is flesh
and what is born of spirit is spirit."
Hear me, my Saviour, as I confess
the ways I live by the flesh,
and turn away from your Spirit,
following the ways of the world,
rather than the greater truth of your way.
Hear me. *(silence)*

I hear your words that God loved this world so much
that you were sent to live among us.
Hear me, my Saviour, as I ask for your forgiveness,
trusting the love that opens the way of life to me
for your compassion is greater than any of my sins.
Hear me. *(silence)*

***

God of goodness and life,
we gather in the hope and beauty of this day,
to be further opened
along the pathways of faith
you set before us.
Holy One,
be our journey and destination.

Question our safe decisions.
Prod our imaginings,
and walk boldly beside us into the unknown,
yet promise-filled, future.
Holy One,
be our journey and destination.
Amen.

***

Offer these words from a place where the reader is heard but not seen. Introduce the assurance of pardon by saying, "Hear the words of Christ."

Thank you for talking with me,
and I have listened to your questions and concerns.
You have heard my words
and my word to you is:
you are forgiven.
For I have been sent into the world
not to condemn it but to save it
and I have come to save you, my child.
Receive this forgiveness
and may my spirit birth new life within you.

***

Hear the deep yearning of our heart, O God!
Open in us the ways of genuine compassion.
For we live in a world of huge and confusing contrasts:
beauty and ugliness,
generosity and impoverishment,
hope and despair,
honesty and deception.

How are we to make sense of all this
and navigate our way through it?

We simply turn to you,
seeking in the stillness –
in the refuge and gift of silence –
your presence; calm, beckoning voice,
and renewing perspective.
Guide us in our prayer,
strengthen us in our action
for this community, nation, and world. *(silence)*

In the faith, hope, and love of Christ we pray,
Amen.

***

Based on Psalm 121:5–8
God is your guardian, your shade.
God remains by your side.
By day the sun will not harm you,
nor the moon at night.
God enfolds your comings and goings,
now and into unknown yet hopeful futures.
Friends,
go from here in peace
to love and serve the God of all grace
in all whom you meet
along life's winding and unfolding roads.
Amen.

Lent 3

LECTIONARY READINGS

Exodus 17:1–7
Psalm 95
Romans 5:1–11
John 4:5–42

God, our Rock, your love revives our thirsting souls. Restore us so that, renewed by your grace, we may be strengthened to bring others to the living water given to us in Jesus Christ our Lord. Amen.

***

Teach a small group of people to lead the response lines and actions below. Invite young children in the group to copy the actions without saying the lines.

Response:
Come *(gesture to folk around you to come close)*
let us worship *(place hands together as if praying)*
and bow down *(bow head).*

In the driest desert, God provided a rock
that held a fountain for those who thirst. **Response**
In a helpless world, at the right time,
God sent Jesus to die for the ungodly. **Response**
In a place of quarrelling, God provides an answer
that holds life for those who hope. **Response**
In a place of wonder, God provided living water,
for those who met there. **Response**
In this place of gathering, God provides the grace
that surrounds those who wait. **Response**

***

One: God of our journeying,
God of dead-ends, U-turns,

and radical new beginnings;
here we gather,
confident only of your attentive and believing love.

Two: Holy One,
commune with us.
Create streams of
love and kindness within us.
Amen.

***

One: Thank you, God, for the gift of Jesus
All: **whose unending life and unconditional love transform our lives.**

One: Thank you, God, for the gift of your Holy Spirit
All: **that leads us into truth and enlightens us on our way.**

One: Like the woman at the well, we all do wrong. May we, like her, have the courage to bring all of who we are in and what we do into the light of your healing love. In a moment of silence, we ask God to bring to mind one thing for which we need God's forgiveness.

Silence.

All: **Loving God, we ask for forgiveness.**

One: In a moment of silence, we ask God to bring to mind someone we have hurt or neglected.

Silence.

All: **Loving God, we ask for forgiveness.**

One: In a moment of silence, we ask God to guide our actions and interactions.

Silence.

All: **Holy Spirit, show us the way. Amen.**

***

One: God, you know us: you know our past and present, and you hold our future. You know the parts of us that we find difficult to accept, the things we struggle to let go of, and the steps we would rather not take. We thank you for your acceptance, for your spirit at work within us and amongst us, and for the all-encompassing love of your son Jesus. Renew our willingness to follow you. Keep our hearts open to your love and to your spirit of truth.

All: **We thank you, God, that we are accepted, forgiven, and free. Amen.**

***

This is a meditative prayer where the sound of pouring water after each petition enables people to engage Jesus as the Living Water.

When we quarrel, hear us, O God.
When our faith in you is thin,
and we turn on each other, we thirst for unity.
Forgive our words that hurt, O God,
and may we drink again from the water of life.
(Pour water into a bowl.)

In our prejudice, hear us, O God.
When our insecurities
bring on a fear of others, we thirst for trust.
Forgive our narrowness of grace, O God,
and may we drink again from the water of life.
(Pour water into a bowl.)

In our hurt of others, hear us, O God.
When we sum people up on hearsay,
rather than meet them in their living, we thirst for honesty.
Forgive the gossip we believe, O God,
and may we drink again from the water of life.
(Pour water into a bowl.)

***

And God says: I am listening to you.
Now hear my words to you.
I am the water of life, come to me all who are thirsty
and you will drink of the living waters
and never be thirsty again.

***

These reflections should be presented by a woman. Following each reflection, sing or play an appropriate song, during which time the woman takes a drink of water from a pitcher with a ladle. She then moves to a different space to continue.

It is a lonely place sitting on the edge,
and there I was on the edge of the well,
not daring to look at him,
but watching his reflection.
He was looking at me.
I knew I shouldn't have,
but I turned to look at him.
He quickly looked away
to stare at the water in the well
and scooped some of it up as if playing with it,
letting it run through his fingers.
Without looking at me he spoke,
"You'll always be thirsty, you know."
Of course I knew,
but I also knew he wasn't talking about water.
He was talking about love.
God, quench the thirst of those who long
to be included, to be part of a family,
to be loved,
those who sit on the edge because there is nowhere else to sit.
May they sit here
and may we be found with them.
(Takes a drink and moves to a new location.)

It is a lonely place being on the edge,
and there I was
on the margins of the community –
the despised gender of a despised peoples.
Yet he just sat there.
He made a point of noticing me
and at first I imagined it was some dare
or some service he required.
I couldn't work it out at first,
but the longer he sat there
the easier it became
and I enjoyed his presence.
It was as still as the surface water at the well.
My soul was calmed,
my faith grew by the edge of the water.
God, touch the voice within us that has been silenced;
voices of justice and inclusion,
voices of love extending into the margins.
Sit with us and empower us
to be your strong witnesses in this world.
(Takes a drink and moves to new location.)

It is a lonely place sitting on the edge,
and there I was on the edge of life,
and the stranger knew how much on the edge I sat.
He knew me well –
a prophet!
And we conversed and spoke of religion,
and faith and ancestors
and I was longing for the Messiah.
He said, "I am he."
Now I knew too much.
God, when we long for the Messiah,
may we find you in the faces of strangers
and in the least expected places.
Give us the courage to search
in the dark places of our lives
and in the unknown places beyond ourselves

where we will hear you say,
"Here I am, the One you are longing for."
(Takes a drink and exits.)

***

One: Your grace flows into us;
All: **may the new life that flows into us also flow through us.**
One: Your truth frees us;
All: **help us to free others.**
One: Your love brings us into life;
All: **hallow our loving and our living.**

Lent 4

LECTIONARY READINGS

1 Samuel 16:1–13
Psalm 23
Ephesians 5:8–14
John 9:1–41

Once we were in darkness,
but now we live in the realm of light.
Once we were in death,
but now we live in the gift of life.
Once we were in bondage,
but now we live in the truth of freedom.
Once we walked in the valley,
but now we live in green pastures.
We come to worship the love that knows no limits,
and opens our eyes to focus on the light.

***

God of soulful love –
a love that finds us and lifts us
in the most confusing and despairing of times –
with gratitude we enter this sacred space,
not to remain as we are or have been,
but to be led somewhere new.
Shepherd us.
Hold us.
Carry us homewards into the heart of Love.

***

God of light,
We give thanks for the physical light and warmth that brighten our lives:
the sun that rises and sets and offers us day and night;
the moon that waxes and wanes and notes the passage of time;

the stars that illuminate the sky
and by which we measure space and mark the seasons.

Thank you for the gift of seeing:
for the beauty we sense with our eyes;
for the insights we perceive as we listen and learn;
for the ability to reason and think ahead.

God of darkness,
we give thanks for times and places where rest and growth can happen:
the nighttime when we can sleep and be refreshed;
the earth where seeds lie dormant and animals hibernate undisturbed;
the womb where new life can grow in safety.

God of darkness and light,
we confess that:
We have sometimes ignored the insights we should have heeded,
or used our perspective for selfish gains.
We have tried to force growth when we should have respected the darkness,
or chosen to stay in a comfortable place
when we could have exposed our lives to the gentle scrutiny of your love.
We own that sometimes life has seemed like a deep ravine
and we could not find your presence near us.
We seek assurance of your goodness and mercy,
wherever we may be on life's journey.
(Short time of silence.)

***

One: Hear these words from scripture:
"O sleeper, Awake!
Rise from the dead, and Christ will shine on you."
So, forgiven and renewed,
receive the light and love of God in Christ
and live in the new life of the Spirit.

All: **We open our hearts to God's love,**

our minds to God's wisdom
and our wills to God's directing.
Amen.

***

Shepherding God,
we are painfully aware
of how imperfectly love is expressed within our world.
So, in trust, we turn once more to you.
In your goodness and mercy, hear the prayers of our hearts:
We are alive to your imaginings
for a new world
and ready to make
a creative difference *(pause).*

For while we do see good and hopeful change,
we also witness violence and dysfunction
whereby the most innocent and vulnerable
continue to be forgotten, abused,
or treated as of no account.
In your goodness and mercy, hear the prayers of our hearts:
We are alive to your imaginings
for a new world
and ready to make
a creative difference *(pause).*

Daily we see and read of the failures
of those in principal positions of care
whose treatment of patients, parishioners, clients, spouses, and children
leave us feeling ashamed,
yet also mindful of our own shortcomings.
In your goodness and mercy, hear the prayers of our hearts:
We are alive to your imaginings
for a new world
and ready to make
a creative difference *(pause).*

Change us, O God.
Create within the desire and capacity
for a love that can gently hold yet let go,
that encounters all others with deep respect,
and is concerned with others' well-being above personal interest.
In your goodness and mercy, hear the prayers of our hearts:
We are alive to your imaginings
for a new world
and ready to make
a creative difference *(pause).*

***

Once you were in darkness,
now we will live as children of the light.
Awake, rise from the dead.
We will go in the light of Christ.
Once you walked through the shadowed valley,
now we are led to green pastures.
Awake, rise from the dead.
We will go in the light of Christ.
Once you were blind,
now we witness to Christ the Lord.
Awake, rise from the dead.
We will go in the light of Christ.

Lent 5

LECTIONARY READINGS

Ezekiel 37:1–14
Psalm 130
Romans 8:6–11
John 11:1–45

Enlivening God, you bring life to dry bones and weary hearts. We cry out from the depths – help us! Pour your Spirit in our hearts so that, trusting in your power to forgive and restore, we may rejoice in the hope you set before us. Amen.

***

O God, we draw near to you
in our joy and our suffering,
our play and our work,
our celebrations and sorrowings.
From the bottom of our hearts we cry,
we delight in your steadfast love.

If you would remember our wrongdoings
we would be bent over with guilt,
but forgiveness is in your heart
and you honour us with your love.
From the bottom of our hearts we cry,
we delight in your steadfast love.

We wait for your presence
and hope to hear your word come to life;
we wait expectantly like the dawn piercing through the night,
like rain in the heat of the day.
From the bottom of our hearts we cry,
we delight in your steadfast love.

***

God of Jesus, who shared our humanity, keep us company on this Lenten journey so that we may find the path to life. Amen.

***

One: Life-giving God,
like Martha, Mary, and Lazarus, we are loved by you.
We think of this family and the way they opened their home to others,
providing care and companionship to Jesus and his friends.
We pray for our homes,
that they may be places where others can find life-giving relationships.
All: **Spirit of God, breathe new life in us!**

One: Also like Martha, Mary, and Lazarus, we are different from one another.
Martha was practical and clear about what she believed.
Thank you for those who use their skills and abilities to care for others.
We pray that their faithfulness and dependability will bring hope
to those who are not sure of their faith and find it hard
to believe in you and in other people.
All: **Spirit of God, breathe new life in them!**

One: Mary loved deeply and felt the pain of loss and desertion.
We pray for those who have experienced the loss of those they love,
those for whom relationships have brought disappointment,
those whose trust has not been honoured.
May they find comfort in their sadness and courage to reach out again to others.
All: **Spirit of God, breathe new life in them!**

One: Lazarus faced illness and death.
Pray for all who face life-threatening illness or injuries,
those paralyzed by fear or anxiety,

and those for whom depression or difficulties make life painful
or seem not worth living.
Help us to face our mortality,
knowing that there are limits to our energy
and there will be an end to our life and strength,
but never an end to your loving presence.

All: **Spirit of God, breathe new life in us!**

One: In a short time of silence we bring our own prayers to God.

Silence.

One: As we finish this time of prayer, we ask:

All: **Spirit of God, breathe new life in us!**

***

One: We cried to God from the depths

All: **and God heard our voice.**

One: We came with our burdens, bound by our fears,

All: **and stand redeemed.**

One: We leave this place with hope

All: **released to serve a living God.**

One: Go in the strength of God who shows steadfast love,
in the courage of Christ who shares our humanity,
and in the companionship of the Spirit who gives life.

Lent 6

Palm/Passion Sunday

LECTIONARY READINGS
(for the Liturgy of the Palms)
Matthew 21:1–11
Psalm 118:1–2, 19–29

(for the Liturgy of the Passion)
Isaiah 50:4–9a
Psalm 31:9–16
Philippians 2:5–11
Matthew 26:14—27:66 *or* Matthew 27:11–54

God of mercy, gird our hearts to be wholly present to the events of Jesus' final days. Open our hearts to sing your praise, and use our tears to water lives committed to working for your reign on earth. In Christ. Amen.

***

*Ask those who are able to gather outside the worship space for this call to worship. Give everyone a palm branch prior to the service. Invite people to wave their branches and say, "**We will rejoice and be glad in it!**" whenever the leader says, "This is the day God has made."*

Open the doors of this holy place,
that we may enter and give thanks to God
for this is the day God has made.
We will rejoice and be glad in it!
(Wave palm branches.)

God has opened the doors of grace
and all creation is invited to join in praise
for this is the day God has made.
We will rejoice and be glad in it!
(Wave palm branches.)

Blessed is the One who comes in God's name
to shed light on our darkness
for this is the day God has made.
We will rejoice and be glad in it!
(Wave palm branches.)

***

Hosanna Saviour,
We wave our palms and sing our praise
as we remember your
triumphal entry into Jerusalem.
May your Spirit enter
the heart of our worship this day,
giving us the strength
to endure the journey which is ahead.

***

Use the prayer invitations below to guide people in their prayers. Provide space for people to offer their petitions either out loud or silently. Conclude by saying, "We pray to you, O God," followed by the shared response, ***"Save us, O God."***

Compassionate God,
We lift our palms of praise with those who first sang out,
"Hosanna to the Son of David!"
Like them, each hand that holds a palm
has a heart that holds a story –
a story of pain, of disappointment, of sorrow.
We share those stories with you now. *(Pause.)*
We pray to you, O God,
save us, O God.

Prince of Peace,
You came in humble obedience
and walked the path of enduring love
even in the face of violent rejection.

We confess that it is difficult
to follow your path of peace,
and the violent road of abuse and war
is all too familiar to us.
We long for your peace, O God. *(Pause.)*
We pray to you, O God,
save us, O God.

Saving God,
We trust in your goodness
and believe your desire
is for all creation
to be held in your redeeming love.
Send us out in your name
to bring comfort to those who mourn,
healing love to those who are sick,
and justice to those who are oppressed.
We wait now for your Spirit. *(Pause.)*
We pray to you, O God,
save us, O God.

***

Arrange to have representatives from different age groups carry the Christ candle around the worship space, relay style, as this affirmation is spoken. One person will begin by lifting the candle from the table and walking some distance. Then someone will rise from her or his seat, take the candle, and walk another length around the worship space. Carry the candle around the space more than once before placing the candle back on the table.

We believe that the Christ
still travels the roads of human life
and is never defeated by our humanness.
We believe that the church
can carry Love wherever we go
and that our dreams of faithfulness
can be given new possibilities in each day.
We believe that, here in this place,

we will find inspiration and encouragement
that will lead us on in our journey with the Christ.

***

Invite people to bring to mind others in need of prayerful support. As they offer their silent prayers, invite them to take a small branch from a basket of branches and place it on a designated "path."

Where in this day do we see the signs
of people trying to carry the life of Christ?
Who needs our prayers and support as they do this?
As a way of offering your prayer,
come and take a small branch and place it on the road
as a sign of loving support.

O God in Christ Jesus,
move in love on this path among us.
Guide your humble people of today, in every place,
as we try to carry faithfully your love.
Warm us with branches of care.
Cool us with gentle leaves
when we are tired or discouraged.
This we pray in your name, Jesus Christ.
Amen.

***

Have someone carry the Christ candle out of the worship space after the spoken bless.

The nights ahead will be long.
We will go in the grace of God.
It will be a bleak time and we may be afraid.
We will go in the grace of God.
It will be a trying time and our faith may be challenged.
We will go in the grace of God.
We go now into suffering and death.
We will go in the grace of God.

SEASON OF EASTER

Easter Day

LECTIONARY READINGS
Acts 10:34–43 *or* Jeremiah 31:1–6
Psalm 118:1–2, 14–24
Colossians 3:1–4 *or* Acts 10:34–43
John 20:1–18 *or* Matthew 28:1–10

Great God of light, you come to us while it is deepest night; God of life, you overcome the power of death. Alleluia! We come from the shadows to stand in your presence, unafraid. Alleluia! Fill our hearts with joy on this day of resurrection. Alleluia! Amen!

***

One: God of life, thank you for the message of Easter:
for the affirmation of your steadfast love;
for the presence of the One who overcame death;
for the promise of life still to be revealed.
All: **Thank you, God of life!**

***

One: Christ is risen!
All: **Christ is risen indeed!**
One: The shadows have gone and the day has dawned!
(Remove black cloth from the worship/sanctuary table.)
All: **Alleluia!**
One: The stone has been rolled away and Christ is alive!
All: **Alleluia!**
One: Our sorrow has turned to joy!
All: **Alleluia!**
One: Christ is risen!
All: **Christ is risen indeed! Alleluia!**

***

One: God of life, thank you for the night:
for those who kept watch through its long hours;
for the gift of sleep, and the refreshment of dreams;
for your faithful presence that keeps us company
when we are not aware of you.
All: **Thank you, God of life!**

One: God of life, thank you for this new day:
for the song of birds, the early morning bustle of city streets,
and the brightening sky;
for this day of all days when we celebrate the risen Christ.
All: **Thank you, God of life!**

***

One: There are alleluias in the air
Two: that skip a beat as they dance over tombs,
One: that push at stones and reveal a saviour,
Two: that explode with a slow beauty in the sunrise,
One: that wake the birds and tear at the dawn.
Two: It is God's special word:
All: **Alleluia!**

One: There are alleluias in the air
Two: that are filled with the voice of God,
One: that are spoken aloud in the chambers of parliament,
Two: that break open hope for the poor,
One: that paint faith with the colour of rainbows.
Two: It is God's special word:
All: **Alleluia!**

One: There are alleluias in the air
Two: that fill every silence with song,
One: that fill every fear with hope,
Two: that fill every injustice with threat,
One: that fill every status quo with conspiracy.

Two: It is God's special word:
All: Alleluia! Alleluia!

***

The objects may be carried into the worship space as they are mentioned and placed in a display.

The crown of thorns has played its part.
It was used to mock Jesus
when the crowd jeered as Jesus made his way to the cross.
But now we laugh with joy,
for the crown of thorns could not weaken love.

The robe has played its part.
It humiliated the dying Jesus
as thoughtless soldiers rolled dice to win it.
But now love wins,
for the robe could not diminish the Spirit of Christ.

The cross has played its part.
It was used to bring suffering and death,
and those who loved Jesus stood beneath it and cried.
But now our tears are dry,
for the cross could not kill love.

The stone has played its part.
It was placed over the tomb of Jesus
to satisfy the fears of the leaders in charge of his death.
But now we celebrate new life,
for the grave could not imprison the Spirit of Christ.

Those things which once played a part in death
have become symbols of resurrection.
In the Spirit of Christ, we know that love
cannot be weakened or diminished, or imprisoned, or killed –
not then, not now, not ever.
Christ is risen!
Christ is risen indeed! Alleluia!

***

Beyond death is abundant life.
We will live it.
Beyond the shadows of hatred and isolation
is the light that draws us into community.
We will follow it.
Beyond the stone covered tomb
is a dance called resurrection.
We will move with it.
Christ is risen!
Christ is risen indeed! Alleluia!
Live in the resurrected Spirit of Christ.

Easter 2

LECTIONARY READINGS

Acts 2:14a, 22–32
Psalm 16
1 Peter 1:3–9
John 20:19–31

Gracious God, your love reaches us through doors bolted by fear and doubt; your life reaches us through wounds and scars. Help us to hear your words of peace and healing; fill our hearts with joy so that we too may confess you as our God. Amen.

***

Spirit of peace, move among us. Breathe trust that relies on your presence when we see and when we don't see. Breathe honesty that acknowledges our doubts and questions. Breathe hope and forgiveness for the sake of community with you and others. Amen.

***

One: Peace to you this day, as you come through open doors.
All: **God's peace to you.**
One: Peace to you who hide behind locked doors.
All: **God's peace to you.**
One: Peace to you who come with more doubt than faith.
All: **God's peace to you.**
One: Peace to you who seek the path to life.
All: **We come, trusting God's goodness and grace.**

***

God of new life,
As we continue to reflect on the happenings of Easter,
renew our joy and trust in you;
encourage our faith
so that although we do not see you,
yet we are able to believe and rejoice in you. Amen.

***

*Invite the congregation to clench their fists tightly during the leader's prayer and then relax their fists during their spoken response. Announce that when the leader says, "Help us to let go now," they are invited to respond, "**We receive your Holy Spirit.**" Read John 20:22–23 as an invitation to prayer.*

Everything we hold on to,
that holds us,
shapes us,
controls us,
and makes us doubt your presence *(pause)*
help us to let go now.
We receive your Holy Spirit.

The memories of hurt,
that speak loudly to us,
that cripple us,
dull us,
and make us doubt your presence *(pause)*
help us to let go now.
We receive your Holy Spirit.

The words that linger,
that have found a home in our reasoning,
that haunt us,
echo in us,
and make us doubt your presence *(pause)*
help us to let go now.
We receive your Holy Spirit.

The acts we have done,
that have hurt and abused others,
that linger in us and hound others,
and make us doubt your presence *(pause)*
help us to let go now.
We receive your Holy Spirit.

***

In every doubt God says,
"Here are my wounds. Touch."
For God is with you in the greatest hurt – calling you.
In every confession you make
God says, "I am listening."
For God is full of grace;
enough for you to let go of all deadly things,
and still be held by the hands of heaven.

***

Invite four people to read a stanza of this prayer. As they do so, have them touch the designated item. After each stanza, light a candle that is situated on a stand near the person who just prayed.

(Touch a wall.)
Touch.
Know what is real.
Barriers that divide:
ethnic cleansing,
sectarianism,
racism.
Touch and know what is real,
and pray for unity.

(Touch the floor.)
Touch.
Know what is real.
The ground on which people walk,
and home to those who have none:
a cold place,
a lonely place.
Touch what is real,
and pray for an end to poverty.

(Touch a door.)
Touch.
Know what is real:
the world one step beyond this place.
Where compassion is needed,
where love searches,
where Jesus walks.
Touch what is real,
and pray for those beyond this place.

(Touch a person.)
Touch.
Know what is real:
those people we share life with;
our family and friends,
our neighbours and community,
our world.
Touch what is real,
and pray for those who journey with us.

***

May you find Jesus standing beside you.
May he be close enough to touch.
May he breathe on all your living,
and speak peace into your lives.
Go now in that peace.
Always.

Easter 3

LECTIONARY READINGS

Acts 2:14a, 36–41
Psalm 116:1–4, 12–19
1 Peter 1:17–23
Luke 24:13–35

God of our journeys, as we follow the way of Jesus who makes sense of our wonderings and our wanderings, open our eyes and our hearts to recognize him in scripture, in our lives, in each other, and when we break bread together. May we live in and share the light of the Resurrection, knowing that we journey with and towards you. Amen.

***

Stand by the Communion table while sharing this call to worship and be prepared to lift the chalice when indicated.

Come, you who love God –
you who speak to God
from the depths of your being –
for God will hear your prayers.
When you are laid low,
God will lift your spirit up.
When you are filled with joy,
God will rejoice with you.
What gift can we offer
in return for God's goodness?
(Lift the chalice.)
We will lift the cup of salvation
and shout, "Hallelujah!" in honour of our God.
For God has brought life from the grave
and refreshed our souls
with abundant life forevermore.

***

O God, we gather with open hearts
ready to receive the new life you give.
Open our eyes, we pray,
that your presence might be revealed
in the community that is gathered here
and the bread that is broken and shared.

***

When all seems lost
and circumstances leave us feeling
empty and afraid;
God of unwavering hope,
may your words of life burn within our hearts.
(silent reflection)

When trust seems impossible
and our eyes remain tightly closed
to the constant breaking in of Spirit;
God of unwavering faith,
may your words of life burn within our hearts.
(silent reflection)

When our spirits feel dry and listless
and where hurt or resentment
creates barriers to human care and friendship;
God of unwavering love,
may your words of life burn within our hearts.
(silent reflection)

***

One: God of all people,
we thank you for the light of Christ's resurrection in which we live.
We thank you for the times you have brought and bring us into new life.
We pray for those suffering from any kind of illness,
and for those paralyzed by grief or sorrow.
We hold them in the light of your love.
All: **Loving God, we call upon you.**

One: God of peace,
we pray for those living in places of conflict and in deprivation.
May we discern and respond to your call on our time,
your call on our resources, your call on our outlook.
All: Loving God, we call upon you.
One: God of new beginnings,
we give you thanks that you travel with us,
that you meet us in people, in places, and in the scriptures.
You surprise us by moments of unexpected revelation.
Grant us the courage and the humility to turn back or away
from paths that we know deep down are not life-giving.
Increase our trust in you, our faith in your word, and our faithfulness in following.
We pray for the church and for communities of faith in all places,
especially those facing a crisis of any kind.
All: Loving God, we call upon you.
One: We pray that our love for one another may be genuine and deep
and extended to all we meet,
especially those who do not know of your life and your love.
We also bring before you those we find difficult to love or like.
We hold up to the light of your love all those who feel that their lives
are without purpose and meaning.
All: Loving God, we call upon you.
One: We give thanks for those who have helped us on our journeys,
for those who have walked alongside us and shown us your love.
We pray for those who have gone before us
and those with whom we share this part of our journey.
All: Loving God, we call upon you. Amen.

***

May Christ who is with us in our joys and sorrows, at all times and in all places, shine the light of his resurrection on the road ahead, surround you with his grace, and uphold you with his peace and purpose for your lives.
Amen.

Easter 4

LECTIONARY READINGS

Acts 2:42–47
Psalm 23
1 Peter 2:19–25
John 10:1–10

Come into this place as you are:
come as friend or stranger;
come as seeker or teacher;
come as old or young;
come as lost or found;
come as you are.
You are the person God loves,
and gives life as the Good Shepherd does:
healing, holding, loving, feeding,
tending, nurturing God.
Come as you are to worship,
and be folded into God's green pastures.

***

Based on Psalm 23

One: God shepherds me and so I lack for nothing.
All: **God lets me rest in peaceful places**
and leads me to quiet pools of refreshment.
God revives me and guides me along true paths.
One: My way may be difficult and fearful,
All: **but I know that God is with me**
and this gives me comfort and courage.
One: God is a bountiful host to me.
All: **God feeds me with abundance,**
while my adversaries look on.
One: God showers me with good things
All: **and God's kindness and love are constantly with me.**
I will always be part of God's family.
Amen.

***

*Announce that when the leader says, "Shepherding God, we have gone astray," the congregation is invited to respond, "**Find us again.**" Some suggestions for projected images are provided.*

Centre yourself.
Seek God in the peace of this place,
and bring to God what you carry,
and all that burdens you.

(Project image of solitary lamb.)
Seek God and give to God
those times you have been left behind,
felt forgotten, ignored, out of touch with others,
that you be made whole again.
Shepherding God, we have gone astray.
Find us again.

(Project image of a sheep standing outside the flock.)
Seek God and give to God
those you have left behind,
forgotten, ignored, passed over,
that they may be made whole again.
Shepherding God, we have gone astray.
Find us again.

(Project image of a flock of sheep.)
Seek God and give to God the hurts,
the prejudices, the acts that keep us from community,
that we may be made whole again.
Shepherding God, we have gone astray.
Find us again.

***

Prepare enough prayer yarns so everyone can have one. Cut white, green, and blue cords (at least 12 cm/5 in in length). Put one yarn of each colour together and tie a knot at one end.

Distribute prepared yarns and safety pins (optional). Invite people to secure the knotted end so the lengths of yarn are free to braid. They may tuck the knotted end in a hymnal or rack in front of them. Or they may pin the knotted end to their clothing.

Mention the colour code below. Invite people to braid or twist slowly the cords together, praying silently for themselves, others, and the Earth as they do so. Play meditative instrumental music.

White – self
Green – others
Blue – Earth

Invite people to come forward and place their braided yarn in an offering plate on a table, or pass an offering plate through the gathered community and have people place their braids in the plate.

Source of All,
may the prayers of our individual hearts
be held together as a common offering of love shared by each
and distributed generously as there is need.

***

Have four voices read this dedication from the four corners of the worship space.

One: All who believed were together and had all things in common.
Two: We will live in balance with the world's needs.
Three: We will possess only love for one another.
Four: What we have is a gift to share with open hands.
One: And they sold their possessions and goods and distributed them to all.
Two: We will live within our needs rather than our means.
Three: In giving life we are given more life.
Four: Our living will be within the fairness and justice of God.
One: Breaking bread in their homes, they partook of food with glad and generous hearts.

Two: We will build community round a table overflowing with God's generosity.
Three: The harvest will be set for the people of the world.
Four: Our food comes from God and we share it in freedom.
One: And God added to their number day by day those who were being saved.
Two: We are braided together in God's grace.
Three: God's love encircles and gathers us.
Four: We are held within the love of God.

***

Into the world,
we will go with God by our side.
Into all life,
we will go with God on our way.
Into every future,
we will go with God in every journey.
For God is waiting there for us,
and we will meet God there.

Easter 5

LECTIONARY READINGS

Acts 7:55–60
Psalm 31:1–5, 15–16
1 Peter 2:2–10
John 14:1–14

Be with us, O God, when we are challenged to account for the hope that your love has placed in our hearts. Open us to the call of your gospel of peace, and make us bold and enduring witnesses to your saving love in Christ. Amen.

***

You are the One to whom we may go. You are the place where we find refuge as well as call. Yours are the hands in which we are held in grace. When trouble comes, may we not be troubled. May we trust you, and the way you travel with us. In Jesus Christ. Amen.

***

Open us, loving God. When we want to close our hearts and minds from the cries of others, from pleas for help and proclamations of justice, open us. Remove our fears, and enliven us with your spirit. Open us, we pray. Amen.

***

Have a basket of stones for people to take one from as they enter. Invite everyone to hold his/her stone and feel its shape and texture as these words are shared together.

One: Like the multi-hued pebbles gathered onto a beach,
All: **so we come from many places.**
One: Like river stones, smooth from life's surges or chipped in the world's torrents,
All: **so we come worn and wounded.**
One: Like precious stones, chosen, crafted, and valued,

All: **so we come cared about and loved by God.**
One: Like the stones of a building,
All: **so God brings us together.**
One: Come, as living stones, into God's presence!
All: **We come to worship God.**

***

Invite everyone to hold his/her stone in open hands, to feel its hardness and weight. There will be a chance to place the stone in a basket towards the end of this prayer of confession.

One: Life-renewing God, we celebrate the events of Easter:
the stone that was rolled aside, opening the way to life;
the risen Christ who took the frightened disciples by surprise;
the one who was rejected becoming the keystone.
All: **Alleluia! Christ is risen!**
One: The small stones in our hands are hard, and stones on a path can hurt our feet.
We think of the challenges in life that make our way hard:
large things that make us change direction and find another path in life;
little things that make us stumble.
All: **We lament the events in life that have dashed our hopes and dreams;**
we confess our annoyance and anger when life has not gone the way we planned.

One: Even a tiny stone in a shoe can cause injury and pain;
and small things in life can take our minds off the way we are going
and spoil the pleasure of travelling.
Narrow attitudes and unrealistic expectations can cause pain for ourselves and others.
All: **We lament the injuries we have borne through others' carelessness;**
we confess the pain we carry when we fail to stop and deal with the things that need to be put right in our lives.

Forgive us for journeying with burdens we do not need to carry.
We commit these stones to you, with all that they represent for us,
and place them in your redeeming love.

Invite those who wish, and are able, to place their stones in a basket or bowl at the foot of the cross, or in some other appropriate place. Alternatively, baskets or bowls can be passed round the seated congregation to collect the stones.

***

We come together in hushed tones,
not out of a tentativeness or reluctance of faith,
but in the realization that following
in the way of Godly love
requires vulnerability and risk.
We rest in the warmth of the Spirit
felt deep within each
and through this community of the all.
We open our hearts
to new possibilities of faithfulness.

***

Jesus, you say we should not
let our hearts be troubled,
but they are;
troubled for this world, this place.

There is a place for those who mourn
and for those who hurt,
a place of comfort and a place of healing:
for those we have lost to illness,
and those we have never known.
In silence we pray for them.
Hear us.

There is a place for those
who hunger and thirst,
a place of banquets and grace:
for those farmers trapped in unfair trade,
those families dispossessed.
In silence we pray for them.
Hear us.

There is a place for those
imprisoned for belief and justice,
a place of freedom and full lives:
for those mothers of the disappeared, those fathers exiled.
In silence we pray for them.
Hear us.

There is a place for those
oppressed and downtrodden,
a place of liberation and justice:
for those children of sectarianism, those families divided.
In silence we pray for them.
Hear us.

Jesus, you say we should not
let our hearts be troubled,
but they are;
troubled for this world, this place.
Hear our prayer.

***

Have those gathered select a stone from baskets that are distributed during the offering collection. Invite them to consider what they would like to give their time and strength to in the weeks and months ahead. They may take the stones home as reminders of this dedication. Invite people to hold their stones as the prayer is spoken.

Embraced by Loving Spirit,
our imaginations hold infinite possibilities
for making real a mission of love.

When we are confronted with hostility,
may we remain firm with courage.
When we are misunderstood and challenged
may we speak our truth in love.
Even as the stones in our hands
have potential for good or harm,
may we continue to use our strength –
as individuals and a community –
for faith-filled purposes.

Easter 6

LECTIONARY READINGS

Acts 17:22–31
Psalm 66:8–20
1 Peter 3:13–22
John 14:15–21

Invite people to blow into their hands after each response line, symbolizing the Spirit within us all. Another option is to have someone play a singing bowl or ring a bell at this time, shaping a different kind of space with sound. The response line is to be read by a different person from a different place in the room each time.

When the way is difficult, and the path is lonely, Jesus says:
I will not leave you alone.

When the journey is smooth, and the travelling easy, Jesus says:
I will not leave you alone.

When the horizon is far, and the call is clear, Jesus says:
I will not leave you alone.

When the place is here, and the time now, Jesus says:
I will not leave you alone.

***

Holy God, as we reflect on the mystery and the miracle
of your presence with us and amongst us,
anchor us in your love,
ground us in your peace,
and open us to the truth and the comfort
of your Holy Spirit, today and always. Amen.

***

Provide everyone with a sheet of paper and a pencil in order to write a short prayer of confession following the shared prayer.

Forgiving One, unseen yet known,
we hear the world speak in power and in greed
and we hear you speak in love and grace.
May our lives be lived in the echo of your voice.

When we are persuaded by the want that leads to hurt,
the hankering that leads to greed,
the yearning that leads to selfishness,
forgive us for following the wrong way
and may we turn again and follow you.

When we are persuaded by the spin that becomes truth,
the belief that becomes dogma,
the fear that becomes intolerance,
forgive us for following the wrong way
and may we turn again and follow you.

Forgiving One, seeing and forgiving,
knowing and loving,
we turn from following the wrong way
and face you with our confessions.
Hear us.
(Pause and give space to write prayers.)

Invite people to take their sheets of paper, tear them up and scatter them on the floor, or throw them into the air.

No one has seen God.
Yet Jesus has shown us God.
Jesus is the assurance of God's forgiveness.
Hear our confession,
as we hear your forgiveness.

God, known and unknown,
forgiving and full of grace,
we turn away from the gods of our culture,
and choose to follow you.

***

God, parent of us all and of Jesus, thank you for your spirit of truth that unites us with you and with Jesus. Thank you that your presence with us is constant. Unite us as one body so that we may support and strengthen one another. Amen.

***

One: Where there are places of fear in our lives,
All: **may they be filled with the Holy Spirit.**
One: Where fear distorts our perspective,
All: **may your Holy Spirit shine light.**
One: Where people live in fear of war, or in the midst of war,
All: **may your Holy Spirit bring comfort.**
One: When your church is afraid to speak out on matters of justice and peace,
All: **may your Holy Spirit move us to speak truth.**
One: God of grace, when we fear your call on our lives,
All: **may your Holy Spirit comfort and reassure us.**
One: When we orphan ourselves from you by controlling and working out of our own authority,
All: **remind us that power and authority rest with you, O God.**

Easter 7

LECTIONARY READINGS

Acts 1:6–14
Psalm 68:1–10, 32–35
1 Peter 4:12–14, 5:6–11
John 17:1–11

God of heaven and earth, we celebrate the Christ who came to live as one of us. We celebrate the Christ who would stop at nothing – not even death – to proclaim God's love for all people. We celebrate the Christ who rose from death to show that there is no end to God's love. And we celebrate the Christ who, in leaving this earth, entrusted to us the task of continuing this work. Amen.

***

Invite two people to stand on opposite sides of the worship space each carrying a lit candle. As they read the words from Psalm 68 and John 17, they walk towards the centre of the worship space and light the Christ candle together.

One: The psalmist says: You, O God,
have taken the lead with your people
when you marched out into the wild.
Two: The gospel says:
Display the bright splendour of your Son,
that the Son may show your glory, O God.
One: Sing, O kings of the earth,
Sing praises to God!
Two: This is eternal life that they know you,
the one and only true God.
One: Call out, "Bravo!" to God,
the High God of Israel.
Two: Jesus glorified you on earth
down to the last detail
of what you had Jesus do.

One: God's splendour and strength
rise huge as thunderclouds.
Two: Glorify Jesus Christ with your glory,
the very glory Christ had before there was a world.
One: O you, God's people, bless God!
Two: As Jesus glorified God on earth.
Both: Let us worship and glorify God.

***

In his final hours, Jesus prayed
for those who would follow him saying,
"All mine are yours,
and yours are mine;
and I have been glorified in them."
May the heart of Jesus beat on in us,
the beloved community of witnesses,
as we devote ourselves
to this moment of worship.
Amen.

***

One: Much time is wasted staring at the sky,
longing for something miraculous to happen,
waiting for God to step out of heaven,
and make everything right.
Two: But the messengers of God say,
"Why are you wasting time looking at the sky?"
Instead, live out your hope in the world as God's people.
Both: May we live in unity,
and with your forgiving grace,
listen to each other's experiences,
and renew our call to love. *(Pause.)*
One: Much time is wasted staring at political leaders,
expecting a snap of the fingers,
waiting for a dictate, a law, an idea,
that will solve the problems of the world.

Two: The messengers of God say,
"Why are you wasting time looking somewhere else?"
Instead, live out God's justice in the world as God's people.

Both: May we live in unity,
and with your forgiving grace,
listen to each other's experiences,
and renew our call to love. *(Pause.)*

One: Much time is wasted staring at dogmas,
searching for answers and meaning,
softening the cross, easing the way of love,
to make life better, and the world richer.

Two: The messengers of God say,
"Why are you wasting time looking at religion?"
Instead, live out your faith in the world as God's people.

Both: May we live in unity,
and with your forgiving grace,
listen to each other's experiences,
and renew our call to love. *(Pause.)*

***

Based on Psalm 68

One: Loving God, parent of orphans and protector of widows,
you have said that it is not good for people to be alone;
you created us with a deep need to love and be loved.
So when we lose someone close to us, it hurts.
It feels like part of ourselves has been torn away.
Our hearts go out to those who have lost their life partners,
to children who have lost their parents
and parents who have lost their children.
We particularly remember… *(insert names of those grieving a loss).*

All: **Thank you that you are with them,
inspire us to do what we can, too.**

One: Loving God, who cares for all people everywhere,
we believe housing to be a basic right

but know of so many who don't have a home of their own.
Some move in with friends or family and face overcrowding,
some sleep rough in parks or under bridges,
some stay in unsafe or insanitary houses
because they have nowhere else to go.
We particularly remember those in ... *(insert names of places where disaster has made people homeless).*

All: **Thank you that you are with them,**
inspire us to do what we can, too.

One: Loving God who provides for all in need,
you have given us an abundant world
but we find it hard to share things fairly;
the rich get richer while the poor get poorer.
Pictures of starving children in developing countries move us
but we sometimes forget the needy in our own communities.
We particularly remember ... *(insert names of local groups in need).*

All: **Thank you that you are with all your people,**
inspire us to do what we can, too.

***

Carry the white pillar candle out of the worship space following the spoken bless.

Joining with all who seek love,
we give witness to the Great Love
that pulses through creation.
Filled with the Spirit of Christ,
we have no reason to look upward,
for we are empowered
to bring healing, justice, and shalom.
May this be our witness.
We go to be Christ ones alive in this world.

Pentecost

LECTIONARY READINGS

Acts 2:1–21
Psalm 104:24–34, 35b
1 Corinthians 12:3b–13
Numbers 11:24–30
John 20:19–23 *or* John 7:37–39

Come, Holy Spirit, come. Breathe upon us and fill us with your gifts. Open us to your guiding in our words and deeds. Fit us for serving in God's holy realm. Amen.

***

Holy Spirit, who came as wind and flames of fire, fan into life the gifts and abilities of people everywhere; unite us in a creative love that includes others, celebrates differences, and brings glory to God.

***

Holy Spirit,
Diverse and varied as we are, you gather us together, like a mother bird stretching wide her wings.
Today we draw strength from your life and energy, and lift our hearts in praise to you. Amen.

***

One: Pentecost God,
thank you for the gift of the Spirit;
for the power and energy the Spirit brings
and for the knowledge that we are not alone.
Nevertheless, sometimes we find it hard to believe in things we cannot see or touch.

All: **We remember the times we have not recognized the Spirit's still small voice,**
the times we have ignored the Spirit's prompting,

the times we have not acknowledged the Spirit's work around us,
the times we have resisted the Spirit's transforming power.
We remember and we are sorry.
Pour out your Spirit anew; blow through us and ignite us once more.
Amen.

***

One: Our God is always making all things new;
our shortcomings are forgotten and we can begin again,
with God's Spirit as our helper.
All: **Thanks be to God! Amen.**

***

We believe in the Spirit who blows through our lives:
unsettling us
stirring us up,
propelling us forward.

We believe in the Spirit who comes as a fire:
warming us,
empowering us,
re-making us.

We believe in the Spirit who frees our tongues:
for talking of God,
for prayer,
for advocacy.

We believe in the Spirit:
the Counsellor,
the Helper,
the Breath of God.
Amen.

***

One: Holy Spirit of God,
the spark of divine love unites us across the divisions of background and ability, language and culture.
Yet the same Spirit makes us different, equipping us with various gifts, calling us to serve in different ways.
Whatever our individual calling, whoever we are, the breath of the Spirit fans into being the qualities of the God-life.
God of love,
we pray for people living where there is hatred and intolerance, violence, and lack of respect, *(especially…)*.
So we pray,

All: breathe on us, Holy Spirit of God;
may our lives show your love.

One: God of joy,
we pray for those who live in fear or depression,
those whose work is all-consuming or who see no prospect of change, *(especially…)*.
So we pray,

All: breathe on us, Holy Spirit of God;
may our lives show your joy.

One: God of peace,
our thoughts and prayers turn to those who live in war zones and places of danger, to those who are troubled by memories of the past or fear of the future, *(especially…)*.
So we pray,

All: breathe on us, Holy Spirit of God;
may our lives show your peace.

One: God of patience,
we uphold to you those whose dreams and visions of a better world seem far from being fulfilled, *(especially…)*.
Help us to work with them and support them.
So we pray,

All: breathe on us, Holy Spirit of God;
may our lives show your kindness.

One: God of goodness,
we hear so much bad news that it is sometimes hard to recognize the good around us, *(such good things as…)*.
So we pray,

All: **breathe on us, Holy Spirit of God;**
may our lives show your goodness.

One: God of faithfulness,
the world is changing so quickly; it is easy to become bewildered or confused by recent developments and people on the move.
Help us to be found loyal and dependable by those around us, *(especially…)*.
So we pray,

All: **breathe on us, Holy Spirit of God;**
may our lives show your faithfulness.

One: God of gentleness,
we think of people and places that are fragile.
Help us to recognize their value and vulnerability and respond in life-giving ways. *(We pray especially for….)*

All: **breathe on us, Holy Spirit of God;**
may our lives show your gentleness.

One: God of self-control, some of us live in a society where we are encouraged to want and own more and more.
Help us to understand how we can live fulfilling lives without always needing to be filled. *(Today we pray for those who go without…because we/others are greedy.)*
So we pray,

All: **breathe on us, Holy Spirit of God;**
may our lives show self-control.

One: Holy Spirit of God,
fan into our being the qualities of the God-life.

All: **Amen.**

***

Through the Spirit of God,
all things live and have their being.
We receive the Spirit
and live in God's way.
Jesus breathes the Spirit upon us
and we are forgiven and forgiving.
We receive the Spirit
and live in God's way.
The Holy Spirit is with us always,
the presence of God in our world.
We receive the Spirit
and live in God's way.

SEASON AFTER PENTECOST

Trinity Sunday

First Sunday after Pentecost

LECTIONARY READINGS
Genesis 1:1—2:4a
Psalm 8
2 Corinthians 13:11–13
Matthew 28:16–20

Gracious God, as we take in the stories of creation, help us to find the places where creation and re-creation are calling out to us. Help us to move with the rhythm of your creation, so that in our care we may find that it is, indeed, good. Amen.

***

One: God has called and fashioned me light.
Two: God has called and fashioned me sky.
Three: God has called and fashioned me life that grows from Earth.
Four: God has called and fashioned me sun and moon and stars for day and for night.
Five: God has called and fashioned me living things in water and air and on land.
Six: God has called and fashioned me humankind, woman and man.
Seven: God has called and fashioned me Sabbath, a day to celebrate.

***

Open to your creation, we come.
Like a wave falls onto its shore, we come.
Like a bird lands in its nest, we come.
Like the first star of the night appearing, we come.
O God, help us to come with open hearts for worship this day. Amen.

***

One: Giver of light, companion in darkness,
be with all who journey in shadows:
who grieve death's coming,
who yearn for hope's renewal,
who seek a way forward.
Let us pray… *(silence)*

Two: God of the sky above,
uphold all who feel as though life and the world are collapsing:
in anxiety, in fear,
in conflicts raging around and within.
Let us pray for… *(silence)*

Three: God of Earth beneath,
grounding us for the sake of growth,
nurture in all that which brings forth good:
acts of peace and justice,
deeds of compassion and love,
hospitality to all in need.
Let us pray… *(silence)*

Four: God of Sun and Moon and Stars,
may we rejoice in the marvels of creation:
mysteries that stretch our imaginations,
beauties that fill our spirits,
for all we have experienced
and for all that still awaits us.
Let us pray… *(silence)*

Five: God of every living creature,
may a deep and deepening appreciation
for all life be renewed with us:
may we care for life as you care for life.
Let us pray… *(silence)*

Six: God in whose image we have been fashioned,

may we value the gift and responsibility
of the environment around us:
delighting in relationship with you,
honouring our kinship with all,
reflecting your goodness.
Let us pray… *(silence)*

Seven: God of Sabbath, we rest in you:
rest that is not an escape from the world,
but a means to enjoy it more fully
enabling us to serve with renewed energy,
refreshed by Sabbath grace.
Let us pray… *(silence)*

***

We believe in God the Creator
who speaks and we live,
who breathes and we are sustained,
who loves and we are renewed.

We believe in Christ the Saviour
who is born and we see light,
who breathes and we have peace,
who touches and we are healed.

We believe in Spirit the Holy One
who comes and we are empowered,
who breathes and we are filled with compassion,
who stirs and we become a new creation.

***

God creates the whole universe
and asks us to care for it with love.
Jesus welcomes us as his sisters and brothers
and asks us to become one family.
The Holy Spirit teaches us how to reconcile

and build a world of peace.
So go to serve the God of many names
and be blessed by the God of many names.
We go in the presence of God.

Sunday between May 29 and June 4 inclusive

(if after Trinity Sunday)
Proper 4 [9]

LECTIONARY READINGS
Genesis 6:9–22; 7:24; 8:14–19
Psalm 46
Romans 1:16–17; 3:22b–28, (29–31)
Matthew 7:21–29

From your love, O God, comes our life. From your grace, O God, comes our future. From your compassion, O God, comes our redemption. Hold us always in your presence, and lead us to live with trust in you. Amen.

***

Based on Psalm 46
Announce that when the leader says, "God says," the people respond, "Be still and know that I am God."

Waters of doubt and fear roar and foam about us and God says,
Be still and know that I am God.
Mountains of power beyond us tremble and God says,
Be still and know that I am God.
Rivers and puddles make us glad the places where God is, and God says,
Be still and know that I am God.
Even now, behold the work that God is doing, and God says,
Be still and know that I am God.

***

We come, O God,
with our eyes and imaginations filled with the hard things of our world.
We come, O God,
seeking promises that offer us hope.
We come, O God,
Seeking inspiration to see your signs, know your healing,
and to be sent forth renewed as your people.

***

In sadness and anger, we daydream
about starting over with a fresh world.
Yet we know you have called your creation
"good" and "very good," O God.
You know when we have lost our memory of good things.
Help us see the things of hope that we no longer can see.
Remind us of the stories of promise when we have let those stories get flooded with our own anxious things.
Return us to our identity as your people in the presence of the Christ.
Amen.

***

God creates us over and over again for new life.
God has promised to hold us as children no matter what.
God forgives us. God renews us.
God promises new life in the midst of our brokenness.

Sunday between June 5 and June 11 inclusive

(if after Trinity Sunday)

Proper 5 [10]

LECTIONARY READINGS
Genesis 12:1–9
Psalm 33:1–12
Romans 4:13–25
Matthew 9:9–13, 18–26

Open our hearts, O God, that we might better understand what it means to live in hope as we follow your leading. Enable us to live with openness to, and trust in, the restoration you bring. In Jesus Christ. Amen.

***

Based on Psalm 33:1–12
Invite a few people, including some children, to repeat a simple response.
Response:
The earth is full *(make a large circle with the arms)* of God's steadfast love *(bring arms to an "X" over the body).*

Rejoice in God, you righteous ones,
for praise looks good on you.
Praise God with instruments
and sing to God with shouts of joy.
Response
God does not speak in vain
but every promise made is a promise kept
and God's work is done in faithfulness.
Response
God truly loves all that is just
and every deed done with a right heart
is a pleasing sight to God.
Response

Happy are all who find life in God,
those who find a home in the heart of love.
Response

***

O God, we know your restoring love through the welcome of a stranger,
the touch of a friend, and the gift of healing and wholeness.
Make us mindful of your love this day
so we might be restored to you and one another.

***

From the arrogance of exclusivity to the inclusive love of community,
restore us, O God.
From the isolation of religiosity to the common fold of faith,
restore us, O God.
From the pain of disease to the hope of healing wholeness,
restore us, O God.
From the haughty seat of judgment to the common table of Christ,
restore us, O God.
From the fear of death to the joy of new life in your spirit,
restore us, O God.

***

Reader One is clearly visible to the congregation and Reader Two is in a place where he or she can be heard but not seen.

One: *Read Matthew 9:9.*
Two: Go and learn what this means: "I desire mercy and not sacrifice."
One: *Read Matthew 9:10–11.*
Two: Go and learn what this means: "I desire mercy and not sacrifice."
One: *Read Matthew 9:12–13.*
Two: Go and learn what this means: "I desire mercy and not sacrifice."
(Pause for silence or sing a verse of an appropriate hymn.)

One: *Read Matthew 9:18.*
Two: Go and learn what this means: "I desire mercy and not sacrifice."
One: *Read Matthew 9:19–22.*
Two: Go and learn what this means: "I desire mercy and not sacrifice."
(Pause for silence or sing a verse of an appropriate hymn.)

One: *Read Matthew 9:23–25.*
Two: Go and learn what this means: "I desire mercy and not sacrifice."
One: *Read Matthew 9:26.*
Two: Go and learn what this means: "I desire mercy and not sacrifice."
(Pause for silence or sing a verse of an appropriate hymn.)

Sunday between June 12 and June 18 inclusive

(if after Trinity Sunday)
Proper 6 [11]

LECTIONARY READINGS
Genesis 18:1–15, (21:1–7)
Psalm 116:1–2, 12–19
Romans 5:1–8
Matthew 9:35—10:8, (9–23)

From the north and from the south,
from the east and from the west,
from *(neighbouring town)* and from *(neighbouring town)*,
God calls us together to worship and serve.

Out of poverty and wealth,
out of health and disease,
out of whatever circumstance in which we live,
God calls us together to worship and serve.

Out of a spirit of jubilation and despair,
out of times of hope and uncertainty,
out of whatever state our heart is in,
God calls us together to worship and serve.

***

You name us, O God,
with grace we do not fully grasp;
for you call us to love as we have been loved.
You send us, O God,
to persons and communities in need;
for you call us to see and respond with compassion.
In following your call,
strengthen us to follow your example in Christ Jesus. Amen.

***

God of compassion and mercy, strengthen our resolve to say yes to your call to love as you have loved us. Send us to form relationships of care and compassion with all who live in need, following the example of Jesus the Christ. Amen.

***

Gracious Host of heaven and earth,
we celebrate your invitation
to worship and serve in your name.
We are honoured by your call
and long to answer in faithfulness.
Yet we confess those attitudes and allegiances which hold us back:
Fear…discouragement…guilt…
laziness…lack of confidence…greed…
self-centredness…lack of compassion…
and all other things that lie in our hearts.
May we hear you speak our names.
We pray you will fill us with courage so we can move forward in faith
and respond with compassionate love.

***

You have been named by God and called by the Spirit of Christ to serve in this world.
Live in faith and proclaim the good news of God.

***

The harvest is large,
but there are not many workers to gather it in.
We are God's servants.
Jesus gathered his followers
and sent them out to change the world.
We are God's servants.
To proclaim the gospel. To heal.
To bring new life. To challenge the forces of evil.
We are God's servants.

Jesus sent them to be his hands, his feet, his voice.
We are God's servants.
Go and serve in the name and power of Jesus Christ.
We are God's servants.

Sunday between June 19 and June 25 inclusive

(if after Trinity Sunday)
Proper 7 [12]

LECTIONARY READINGS
Genesis 21:8–21
Psalm 86:1–10, 16–17
Romans 6:1b–11
Matthew 10:24–39

In our wilderness, God comes and says,
"Do not be afraid for I have heard your voice."
Out of the shadows of fear
and into the light of faith we come, O God.
When we ask for a sign of love,
God comes and provides all that we need.
Out of the shadows of fear
and into the light of faith we come, O God.
The old ways have been put to death
and we are made alive with Christ.
Out of the shadows of fear
and into the light of faith we come, O God.
Jesus says, "Those who find their life will lose it,
and those who lose their life for my sake will find it."
Out of the shadows of fear
and into the light of faith we come, O God.
Come, let us worship in faith our faithful God.

***

Our many storied God,
you give name to the prayers sung through our living.
You created a world with so much potential for beauty.
It is through this world that we experience the many stories that make us who we are.
Help us to encounter you today,
during this time of beholding and wonder.
Amen.

***

Based on Psalm 86

Turn your ear towards us, O God, and speak comfort to us for we come to you in need.
We are completely devoted to you and we trust in you alone to restore us.
Extend your grace and make our hearts be glad for we know you are good and forgiving and we long to live in your steadfast love forever.
Amen.

***

Patient God,
it's true: we don't *want* you to disrupt our peace.
Too often, we don't let you interrupt our comfort and complacency.
We like things the way they are.
We like living based on the economy of *this* world,
rather than *your* economy of love.
Too often we choose the easy route.
We wonder: What are you seeking to teach us?
What are we to learn from you?
Too much of our lives is spent doubting you,
instead of living into your beautiful reminder
that we are heard, known, and loved.
For this, we say sorry, forgive. Amen.

***

Our Divine Caregiver,
you have counted the hairs on our head
and your loving eye is always upon us.
Show us where we might move out with confidence
to speak bravely of your way
even if the consequences seem hard to bear.
(Pause.)
We pray to you, O God,
give us the courage and compassion to live for you.

Holy Sparrow Creator,
you take delight in the smallest creature

and your compassion sustains all of creation.
Conceive your selfless love within our hearts
and birth within us the desire
to give voice where the voice has been silenced.
We pray to you, O God,
give us the courage and compassion to live for you.

Eternal God, we have no reason to fear
for we know that, in life or in death,
we will always belong to you.
Make us mindful of your presence
and help us to live out of this truth
even when the future seems cloudy and uncertain *(pause).*
We pray to you, O God,
give us the courage and compassion to live for you.

***

Jesus, you call us to live our faith, travelling beside you, in a world filled with tension. As you bring peace to the world, you also disrupt our peace – turning our lives upside down. May we be reminded of your constant love for us. May we feel your disturbing presence in our lives as a reminder that we are heard, known, and loved as cherished children of God. Amen.

***

One: God tells us, "Do not be afraid!"
Two: Jesus tells us, "Have no fear!"
Three: Paul tells us, "Death no longer has dominion…"
Four: The psalmist tells us, "God is abounding in steadfast love."

One: Let us go out to our work unafraid.
Two: Let us go out to our ministries, confident that God is with us.
Three: Let us go out to our discipleship in newness of life.
Four: Let us go out to our service with grace and strength.
People: **Where God leads, we go with confidence. Where God sends, we go with faith.**

Sunday between June 26 and July 2 inclusive

Proper 8 [13]

LECTIONARY READINGS

Genesis 22:1–14
Psalm 13
Romans 6:12–23
Matthew 10:40–42

Hospitable God, we offer thanks and praise for the welcome you extend in friendship and forgiveness. Guide us to welcome others through our relationships, our forgiving and accepting forgiveness. Help us grow in the joy of offering and receiving love. Amen.

***

You welcome us, O God, with abundant grace.
Your welcome comes
in community and forgiveness,
in creation's beauty and love's joy.
So may we welcome others:
through our relationships,
in our forgiving and accepting forgiveness,
in the joy of love's offering and receiving.
Amen.

***

One: Welcome to all who are weary, tired, or burned-out.
All: **We come to be refreshed and renewed in God's presence.**
One: Welcome all who are anxious, worried, or burdened.
All: **We come to be calmed and comforted by the Spirit.**
One: Welcome to all who feel complacent, comfortable, or detached.
All: **We come to be stirred by Christ's message for us.**
One: All are welcome here. Come as you are.
All: **Together, we will rest in God's presence,**
be calmed by the Spirit,
and be stirred by Christ's message.
Together we will welcome one another as we gather for worship.

***

Loving God, you graciously welcome and love each of us exactly as we are, and you model how we should be with each other. May you be patient with us and help us as we seek to understand what your true welcome and your hospitality really mean for how we should be in our communities. We pray this in Jesus' name. Amen.

***

One: How long, O God? Will I be forgotten forever?
Two: With these words, the psalmist yearns to be remembered, to be welcomed.
One: Love's touch is known through our hands and spoken through our words.
Two: Divine welcome is expressed through our graciousness,
and remembered by our mindfulness.
All: **Holy God, forgive us**
when we have missed opportunities to offer welcome.
Perhaps we did not see the need.
Perhaps we did not care enough.
May we extend the welcome we receive through your Spirit.
And may we remember that, in the holy act of welcoming others,
we welcome you.

***

While our lives may be mostly settled, and while we may have found a place of welcome here in this community or another, at times we search for deeper welcome. We await the mere recognition of our value, awaiting the simple affirmation: You are a beloved and welcomed child of God. For these times, for all, who still seek a way forward and space to be, let us pray.

We pray, O God, for a spirit of welcome and acceptance
in the community that bears your name.
Open our doors, and hearts, to all who come seeking.
We pray in silence. *(silence)*

We pray, O God, for all who wander without a home
because of economic turmoil, or political unrest,
or social or familial estrangement.
May we be led to places and people who extend hospitality
and touch needs in life-giving ways.
We pray in silence. *(silence)*

We pray, O God, for all who yearn
for cups of cold water to quench thirsts
for water, or relationship, or sacred space.
We pray for health of body,
and peace of mind, and wholeness of spirit.
We pray in silence. *(silence)*

We pray, O God, for those of us and others
who are in positions to offer holy welcome, space, hope,
companionship.
We pray for the compassion and courage
to embody the kind of welcome extended to all through Christ.
We pray in silence. *(silence)*

Sunday between July 3 and July 9 inclusive

Proper 9[14]

LECTIONARY READINGS

Genesis 24:34–38, 42–49, 58–67
Psalm 45:10–17 *or* Song of Solomon 2:8–13
Romans 7:15–25a
Matthew 11:16–19, 25–30

All-wise God, help us to discern the times in which we live, and to live faithfully within them. Bless us as we serve in the responsibilities you gently lay upon our shoulders, and lead us to find our rest and strength in you. Amen.

***

One: We enter worship through doors that have been opened for us:
Two: opened by God's grace that welcomes all;
Three: opened by a community that welcomes everyone.
All: **Let us open the doors of our minds and spirits to Sacred Presence.**
Let us open the doors of our community to all.
Let us open the doors to our kinship with each other and all creation in Christ.

***

Gracious God, you meet us in the most unexpected of places:
in the moments when your presence seems to have disappeared;
in the eyes of a stranger;
in the experiences that make us feel the most uncomfortable;
in abundance that is found amidst perceived desolation.
We come to worship today, giving thanks for the gift of encounter.
Through your Spirit's movement in our lives and in this time together,
may our hearts be torn open to your call in our lives,
so that we may be stirred to go out and transform your world.
Amen.

***

God of new life,
we come to this time and place,
feeling raw and vulnerable.
We know that too often we forget about your constant love;
we look for love in all the wrong places,
and we put our trust and life in all the wrong things.
And yet, we continue to come,
bearing the hope of transformation that is only possible
in and through you. Amen.

***

Through the sound of water,
we hear vibrancy.
Through the touch of water,
we feel calm.
Through the taste of water,
we experience nourishment.
God's living waters are ever-present in our lives,
offering constant love through vibrant, calm and nourishing encounters.

God is a God of abundance and relationship.
And for that we rejoice!

***

Invite people to cup their hands together in their laps as though holding a burden. When they hear the words, "You invite the weary to come, O God" they respond,

> I give you my burden *(while lifting their hands).*
> And I take your love upon me *(fold arms over chest).*

God of all people and places,
in a world of plenty, many are hungry;
in a world of abundance, many are homeless;

in a world of power, many are powerless.
We see the balance of justice tipped
and we know the pain of oppression and unfairness.
Into this world of suffering
you invite the weary to come, O God.
Response

God whose touch can restore and heal,
our bodies testify to the decay of time
and we bear the burden of imperfection and illness.
We take comfort in knowing
that you hear the cries of those with disease,
you stand beside the neglected and shunned,
and you invite the weary to come, O God.
Response

God who knows each heart,
we name silently the concerns and situations
that weigh down our hearts and minds… *(pause).*
You invite the weary to come, O God.
Response

***

Listen! Can you hear it?
It's the sound of the Beloved,
leaping upon the mountains
and bounding over the hills!
Let us go from this place,
open to the Beloved's movement in our lives,
and open to embracing love's beauty in the world.
Go – ready to greet the stories of another as opportunities for love.
And ready to be transformed by God the comforter, God the redeemer,
and God the sustainer. Amen.

Sunday between July 10 and July 16 inclusive

Proper 10 [15]

LECTIONARY READINGS

Genesis 25:19–34
Psalm 119:105–112
Romans 8:1–11
Matthew 13:1–9, 18–23

Psalm 119 is an alphabetical acrostic in which each stanza begins with the same Hebrew letter. This paraphrase resembles this acrostic quality. Read one sentence and then have the congregation repeat it from memory as a way of planting the word in your heart.

A word of yours is like a lamp
    Bringing light to my path.
Complete allegiance is yours, O God,
    Dedicated am I to all of your ways.
Even when hardships come to me
    Faithful will you be in bringing life.
Gifts of praise I offer you, O God,
    Here I stand, a student of your way.
I will hold your words forever before me,
    Joy to my heart they bring.
Keeping your word is my life's ambition.
    Living forever in your way. Praise God!

***

One: To come into Holy Presence is not to come without wonderings about why some things are as they are.
Two: So come to us in our wonderings, God of Rebekah, and companion us.
One: To come into Holy Presence is not to come free of conflict within our lives and relationships.
Two: So come to us in our tensions, God of Esau and Jacob, and untangle us.

***

Holy One,
As we gather for worship this day,
may we come united in your love.
May we seek wholeness in your Spirit.
May we find peace in your presence.
May we absorb the kindness found in our neighbours.
May we come ready.
Amen.

***

Ever-present God, bless us now as we open ourselves to these stories – stories that are sometimes difficult and which hold tensions, lies, and rivalry. May we wander through them with a heart open to the ways that your presence, truth, and love is near. Amen.

***

God of each, God of all:
We pray for our families,
those with whom we are drawn together
by birth or by marriage or by adoption.
May they receive care and love
from you and from us as well.

We pray for our friends and neighbours,
those with whom we are drawn together
by common places of work or learning,
by common aspirations and values.
Strengthen the ties between us,
and may we find in these relationships
the freedom and companionship and community
that nurture us and the world around us.

We pray for our fellow citizens,
those with whom we are drawn together by birthplace and nation,

by regional ties and societal traditions.
Fashion these bonds so to insure
the relationships and ideals we claim
are paid more than lip-service,
so that who we are and have been
never closes us to who we may yet become.

We pray for those who are part of this community
and in the whole Christian Church,
those with whom we are drawn together
by common faith and uncommon grace.
May we thrive in ministry,
may we expand in mission,
may we deepen in spirituality,
and may we grow closer to one another.

We pray for those who are fashioned in your image,
with whom we are drawn together in one family.
Free us to recognize the stranger as no stranger,
but sister and brother;
and to see the joy and need of any
as the cause for our rejoicing and compassion.

***

Hear the promise of God.
Through all these times, amidst all these conditions,
God offers the Spirit's transformative power
for our companion, guide, and hope.
All: Thanks be to God!

***

God of abundance,
You have planted seeds within our hearts;
seeds of compassion, kindness, justice, mercy, and joy.
Thank you for these gifts of faith

and we pray they will take root in our lives.
Where compassion has been planted,
help us to bear good works and service.
Where kindness has been planted,
help us to bear gentle thoughts and deeds.
Where justice has been planted,
help us to bear a striving for fairness.
Where mercy has been planted,
help us to bear forgiveness.
Where joy has been planted,
help us to bear spirit-filled laughter.
We pause now to consider the seed you have planted
in each one of us and pray for it to bear fruit in our lives *(silence).*
O God, you have provided the soil and the seeds
and we are the blossom and the fruit.
Help us to be your faithful fruit in this world.
Amen.

***

There is no judgment on us
for we are rooted in Jesus Christ.
The law of the Spirit of life
has set us free from that which leads to sin and death.
Let our roots go deep into God's love
as we grow in the grace of Christ Jesus,
and are nourished by the Spirit of life.

***

One: Who we are is a given:
we are children of God's creation.

Two: Who we are is also a choice:
will we honour or undermine
the connections that form us?
We are the joy of God's heart,
to be the source of joy for others.

One: Who we will become is a given:
we will be loved of God,
we will be invited into life-giving relationships
with God and with one another.

Two: Who we will become is also a choice:
will we return God's love by living with love;
will we be faithful or despising partners
in the relationships entrusted to us?
Guide us, on the road ahead:
to love, in the example of your love;
to covenant with the care
with which you covenant with us.

Sunday between July 17 and July 23 inclusive

Proper 11 [16]

LECTIONARY READINGS
Genesis 28:10–19a
Psalm 139:1–12, 23–24
Romans 8:12–25
Matthew 13:24–30, 36–43

God of compassion and mercy, we give thanks that you journey with us into the future. Open us to the gifts of your presence, and increase our willingness to follow as you lead. Turn our hearts to find their way home in you. Amen.

***

God of dreams and visions, we enter into moments of stillness and feel your presence. Through relationships – our relationship with you and with others – we know that you are constantly with us. We thank you for your many gifts to us, but especially for the gifts of being named, known, and cherished by you. Amen.

***

God invites us to gather.
We worship the Holy One who is present in all.
God invites us to come as we are
for the sake of who we may yet be.
We worship the Holy One who calls us
to new ways of being and doing.
God invites us to journey in awe and in trust.
We worship the Holy One in our midst
who blesses and commissions us for the good of all.

***

Help us to listen to the groans in our midst, O God:
Creation's groans of labour pains,

our neighbour's groans of loneliness,
the groans that we bring, with trepidation and awe.
We come bringing all of the yearnings that are on our hearts this day.
And we know that you meet us, wherever we are.
Thank you for your ever-constant presence, and companionship along life's journey.
We know that with you, we are never alone. Amen.

***

One: In our good times and in our bad times,
in our ups and in our downs:
All: We confess you are with us, God.
Two: You are in our moments of transformation,
inviting us to new life.
One: When we are running away,
when we are searching for home:
All: We confess you are with us, God.
One: When we are feeling proud and self-satisfied,
when we are wracked with guilt or shame:
All: We confess you are with us, God.
Two: You steady us on new ways.
One: When we are wrestling, when we are striving:
All: We confess you are with us, God.
Two: You accompany us into new faithfulness to your
presence and call.
All: Amen, and Amen!

***

Have ready a container of oil and a large stone set on a protective covering (or in a large flat dish). Have someone read Genesis 28:18 to the congregation. As they do, lift up the container of oil and pour it upon the stone.

Oil has long traditions of use for healing. We pour this oil on this stone, in this place, to remind us that this, too, is the house of God. As we bring our prayers for healing, know that the oil is here. God is here.

For all who struggle with grief or fear,
anger or pain,
hear our prayers…
(silent or spoken prayer)

For all who face a crossroads,
a time of choosing,
hear our prayers…
(silent or spoken prayer)

For all who find it hard to come into the presence of God,
or who have found the church non-receptive and ungracious,
hear our prayers…
(silent or spoken prayer)

For all on journeys home,
for all setting out on new ways,
for all who feel trapped and unable to move,
hear our prayers…
(silent or spoken prayer)

May Spirit be poured on us all.
(Pour oil upon the stone again.)

***

We woke up this morning and your Spirit was already stepping and twirling to a joyful new song of the day ahead. We woke up this morning and your Spirit was already at the drum, sounding a vibration of justice broadly beneath the surface of human community. We give praise to your Holy Name; may it be praise in all things.

You know how we feel, Wise Creator. While we are asleep evil sometimes undoes our best efforts toward healing, and sows seeds of hatred and insecurity. We come to you with all the vulnerability surrounding us and within us. And sometimes while we are asleep your Mystery has taken hold in ways we couldn't have imagined, surprising us and humbling us. For that we give thanks and take a deep breath to let that surprise take hold of us deep inside. *Silence.*

We ask for your guiding care as we seek safety for all to be able to reveal our true selves and declare what is hard to talk about. Receive our attempts at patience; our attempts to receive those who are different from us; our attempts to keep our ears perked to hear all the voices in your word; to hear the voices of others through your word; and to hear the voices within us disclosed by your word. *Silence.*

***

As you go from this place,
may God's love hold you,
may God's light guide you,
and may God's liberation free you.
Go out into the world reminded of God's unwavering presence in your life, and the lives of others.
May you be reminded of this in the eyes of each person you meet, a reminder of God's love manifest in the world.
Amen.

Sunday between July 24 and July 30 inclusive

Proper 12 [17]

LECTIONARY READINGS
Genesis 29:15–28
Psalm 105:1–11, 45b, *or* Psalm 128
Romans 8:26–39
Matthew 13:31–33, 44–52

Surprising God, is your presence like yeast, or engulfing weeds, or reckless investment, or indiscriminate fishing? As we ponder your reign among us, demand our attention and inspire our service. Alert and revitalized, we thank you. Amen.

***

God of promise, persist in opening our hearts and minds to your presence among us. Send your Spirit to increase our faith and our delight in your surprising ways. Amen.

***

A weaving of Psalm 105 and Romans 8

Glory in God's name, and seek God's presence continually.
God helps us in our weakness,
even when words for prayer escape us.
Give thanks to God, sing songs of praise,
tell of the Holy One's wonderful works.
We trust in the power of God's love to bring good.
Remember: the Holy One keeps covenant
with us and with all.

***

For this prayer, invite people to pray with their eyes open, and with their heads raised. Invite them to place their hands lightly on their thighs, with their palms open upwards – as a symbol of openness to the Spirit.

One: Gracious God, Gentle Spirit, Christ Jesus:
We have come to worship today with all of who we are.
Some of us come feeling uncertain about the relationships and friendships we have with one another.

All: **We give thanks that we can trust in our relationship with you.**

One: Some of us come thinking of past hurts, betrayals, and broken promises in our lives.

All: **We give thanks that we can trust you will never break your promises with us.**

One: Some of us come joy-filled, hopeful, and ready to celebrate.

All: **We give thanks that you journey with us in our moment of joy.**

One: Some of us come reflecting on struggles, sorrows, and dreams.

All: **We give thanks that you accompany us in our struggles.**

One: We come with
different feelings,
different thoughts,
different joys,
different struggles,
and many uncertainties,
and yet we have all come to this place at this time.
(Invite a time of silent reflection and prayer.)

One: For all of these prayers both spoken and unspoken, we give thanks.

All: **Amen.**

***

Gracious God,
we are people of good intentions.
We have good intentions to love one another;
good intentions to be an authentic community together,
to honour our words and promises,
and to always honour you.
We confess that we have not always lived up to our good intentions.
We are broken peoples, and we have broken promises.
Forgive us, dear God, for the ways in which we have failed one another,
and the ways in which we have failed you. Amen.

***

Hear the good news: God forgives us again and again.
We have second chances
and third chances
and fourth chances…
to keep trying to get it right – and to live up to our good intentions.
Even though we sometimes fail God, God never fails us;
God always keeps God's promises to be faithful. Thanks be to God.

***

Invite people to sigh after offering the response line each time. Lead this sigh with your hands by drawing your hands outward as you breathe in and then opening your palms up as you sigh.

One: God, your Spirit intercedes with sighs too deep for words.
Two: We pray for the needs of those whose labours go unrewarded: by layoffs; by loss of benefits; by the devaluing of their worth through the loss of vocation.
All: **Hear our prayers, hear our sighs for love that can work good from ill** *(sigh)*.

One: God, your Spirit intercedes with sighs too deep for words.
Three: We pray for the needs of those who grieve:
the loss of a loved one or friend; the loss of hope; the loss of justice.
All: **Hear our prayers, hear our sighs for love that can work good from ill** *(sigh)*.

One: God, your Spirit intercedes with sighs too deep for words.
Four: We pray for the needs of those who experience estrangement: within family; among colleagues; within and from this community.
All: **Hear our prayers, hear our sighs for love that can work good from ill** *(sigh)*.

One: God, your Spirit intercedes with sighs too deep for words.
Five: We pray for the need of peace where there is war;
for justice where there is inequity; for understanding where there is ignorance and bigotry; for the healing of creation from the ravages of pollution and abuse.

All: **Hear our prayers, hear our sighs for love that can work good from ill** ***(sigh)*****.**

One: God, intercede by your Spirit for us;
intercede by your Spirit through us;
intercede with love for us and through us that transforms life for your good. Amen.

Sunday between July 31 and August 6 inclusive

Proper 13 [18]

LECTIONARY READINGS
Genesis 32:22–31
Psalm 17:1–7, 15
Romans 9:1–5
Matthew 14:13–21

All whose stomachs are rumbling,
who long for a basic meal that satisfies,
enter this space and cry out to God.
We come to you, O God,
trusting in your all-sufficient love.
All whose hearts are filled with grief,
who seek comfort for sorrow spoken and unspoken,
enter this space and cry out to God.
We come to you, O God,
trusting in your all-sufficient love.
All who are searching for justice,
who grieve at the unfairness of this world,
enter this space and cry out to God.
We come to you, O God,
trusting in your all-sufficient love.
All who desire to grow deeper in faith,
who want to know and be known by God,
enter this space and cry out to God.
We come to you, O God,
trusting in your all-sufficient love.

***

As you have always been
with those who have drawn apart;
for solitude, for grieving, for prayer,
out of fear or out of hope:
Be with us now.
As you have always been

with the ones who search or flee;
the ones who struggle or hunger:
Be with us now.
As you have always been
in this place of worship;
and in every place where those who sought you
have encountered you:
Be with us now.

***

Read Matthew 14:13a, ending with "…by himself."
Let us pray for all who grieve;
the death of loved ones and friends,
the victims of war and violence, abroad and at home:
(silent or spoken prayers)

Read Matthew 14:13b ending with "But when the crowds heard…"
Let us pray for all who are searching:
for meaning, for help,
for reconciliation, for peace:
(silent or spoken prayers)

Read Matthew 14:14.
Let us pray for all who are ill;
those who are undergoing treatments;
those who are hospitalized or in care centres
or confined to their homes:
(silent or spoken prayers)

Read Matthew 14:15.
Let us pray for all who hunger, for nourishment of body or
spirit or both;
we pray for those who are homeless,
and for those whose journeys or work take them away from home:
(silent or spoken prayers)

Read Matthew 14:16–18.
Let us pray for the mission of the church;

for openness to opportunities for service,
for trust of Christ's call,
for embodiment of Christ's compassion:
(silent or spoken prayers)

Read Matthew 14:19–21.
Let us celebrate the blessings of God's grace;
let us give thanks to God.
(silent or spoken prayers)

***

God, when we are hungry, feed us with bread and fish for the journey.
When we struggle, sustain us with words of wisdom and stories of hope.
When we wrestle with unknown forces, touch us with companionship and love. Amen.

***

Sometimes, God, we avoid you
because we do not want to wrestle with those things weighing on our hearts,
we do not want to deal with those things we know we are called to address:
those with whom we have broken trust;
those suffering from avoidable circumstances;
those whom we fail to stand up for;
those with whom we avoid eye contact.
When we fail to spend time with you, we fail to learn about ourselves.
Forgive us. Amen.

***

God, grant us the serenity
to accept the things we cannot change,
the courage to change the things we can,
and the wisdom to know the difference. Amen.
Attributed to Reinhold Neibuhr

Sunday between August 7 and August 13 inclusive

Proper 14 [19]

LECTIONARY READINGS
Genesis 37:1–4, 12–28
Psalm 105:1–6, 16–22, 45b
Romans 10:1–15
Matthew 14:22–33

God of endings and new beginnings, we encounter you amidst a broken world. You invite us into these spaces of broken-ness – into these cracks, through which the light shines. Thank you for the gift of your presence, even through the difficulty of the unknown and uncomfortable. Amen.

***

One: We call you our mother.
Two: We call you our father.
Three: We call you our friend.
All: **From many directions, we greet you, O God of many names.**
One: We call you listener.
Two: We call you prophet.
Three: We call you healer.
All: **From many directions, we greet you, O God of many names.**
One: We call you steady.
Two: We call you disturbing.
Three: We call you compassionate.
All: **From many directions, we greet you, O God of many names.**
One: No matter what we call you,
Two: and no matter where we meet you along life's journey,
Three: we know:
All: **Our many-named God calls to us and whispers our names.**
We come to worship in community,
accompanied by a love too deep for words.

***

If we understood everything about you, God,
we would shrink into you and no longer seek you.
So we look for tiny pieces of your cloak of wonder.
We marvel at what comes before us
and hope for a pattern to someday emerge.
We seek your strength, God.
Some days we realize that you use
even our doubt and feelings of being far away
to spin greater glory in creation.
Some days we realize you use
even the suffering of your beloved to deepen peace.
We seek your strength, God.
Some days we wish for burning bushes in the desert
and instead you nudge us to scrounge
for a hint of meaning in our daily activities.
We give thanks for these misty traces of the holy,
for your dewy breath on the windowpane
as we look out into our world.
We seek your strength, God.

***

There are times when we feel cast down,
in deep places, abandoned.
Come to us, O God, when fear overtakes us.
Companion us with your love and presence.
There are times when we lash out in anger,
seeking revenge.
Come to us, O God, when fear controls us.
Companion us with your forgiveness and mercy.
There are times when we come to our wit's end,
not knowing where to turn.
Come to us, O God, when fear disorients us.
Companion us with your plans for good.
In this time, let us open our selves and our fears to God,
in the hope of transformation and a way forward.
(silent prayer)

***

God does not abandon us in our fear
for ourselves or of others.
God comes to us, God journeys with us
– and God can be trusted even when all seems lost.
Thanks be to God!

***

One: Let us pray and let us work
for the dream of God's promised realm;
Two: for all among and beyond us who grieve the death
of loved ones, or beloved relationships:
May peace and comfort be found
in Spirit and acts of human caring.
Three: How beautiful are the dreams that bring and embody good news. *(silence)*

One: Let us pray and let us work
for the dream of God's promised realm;
Two: for all without food or clean water,
and who are our kin in Christ:
That God's justice and our advocacy
might bring the good God intends.
Three: How beautiful are the dreams that bring and embody good news. *(silence)*

One: Let us pray and let us work
for the dream of God's promised realm;
Two: for the strengthening of peacemakers,
for the undermining of those
who rely on violence and meanness of spirit:
That God's shalom and our witness
to the Prince of Peace may be done
for the sake of innocents and all creation.
Three: How beautiful are the dreams that bring and embody good news. *(silence)*

One: Let us pray and let us work
for the dream of God's promised realm;
Two: for faithfulness in our calling
to be Christ's body,
for trust of God evidenced in our budgets
as well as our statements of faith:
That others may discern the love of God
at work through us, imperfect as we are,
and God's strength be revealed even in our weakness.
Three: How beautiful are the dreams
that bring and embody good news. *(silence)*

***

Go out from this place, open to the brokenness in your midst. Go out, ready to answer, "I am here, God; I will not close my eyes, or ignore the difficult truths that you long for me to see."

As you go, know that the love of God surrounds you, the peace of the Christ empowers you, and the fellowship of the Spirit moves within you, and all of creation, now and always. Amen.

Sunday between August 14 and August 20 inclusive

Proper 15 [20]

LECTIONARY READINGS
Genesis 45:1–15
Psalm 133
Romans 11:1–2a, 29–32
Matthew 15:(10–20), 21–28

Wise and loving God, when relationships are fractured, journey with us in the life-giving process of reconciliation. Fill us with patience and unconditional love, so that we might forgive as we have been forgiven. In Christ. Amen.

***

Turn your face toward us, God,
so we might learn again your forgiveness.
Turn your face toward us, God,
so we might learn to forgive ourselves.
Turn your face toward us, God,
so we might learn to forgive one another.

***

Have someone demonstrate and lead the actions of this body prayer. Invite people to stand if they are able, or the actions can be adapted if people remain seated.

(Start with hands over heart.) God, we come each from our own heart journeys to this space, to encounter you and each other.

(Move arms and hands to the sides and palms facing up.) God, we greet this new day, as we are open to all the potential it holds, and open to the community that surrounds us.

(Move arms up above head.) God, we reach for the sky and gather your love.

(Face palms to the ground and push from above head to just above the ground.) We push down and release all the tensions that keep us from being fully present to this time of worship, *(bending down, move hands in circles, palms still facing down, just above the ground)* and we gather energy from all the things that ground us here.

(Stand again and move hands back over heart.) This time together God, we know, is a part of our heart story. Amen.
Do one or two more times together without words.

***

Before worship, place a pitcher of water and a large bowl on a table in the front of the worship space. Pour some water into the bowl before each petition of the prayer.

As we pray, may the water we pour today represent the tears shed of both our suffering and our burden of knowing we've done harm.
Let us pray.
(Pour water.) Giver of all life,
we shed tears of loss for the ways
we have harmed ourselves with harsh self-talk,
words, and behaviours that injure.
God use our tears to water something new.

(Pour water.) Redeemer of all life,
we shed tears of hurt for the ways
we have done harm and received harm
in our families, with our co-workers or schoolmates,
with friends and neighbours,
and with members of this faith community.
God use our tears to water something new.

(Pour water.) Sustainer of all life,
we shed tears for the way we live
in the legacy of dishonour and injury in our culture
in which differences of race, gender, religion, class,
ethnicity, and sexual orientation cause brokenness.
God use our tears to water something new.

(Pour water.) Giver of all life,
we shed tears for the wars of weapons,
words, and ideas that continue between nations and peoples,
taking lives and hopes.
God use our tears to water something new.

***

Our Holy Friend,
we gather this day as your people,
seeking hope amidst the hardships of this world.
We know that sometimes we are overshadowed by fear,
by persecution, greed, hatred, and sadness.
God help us to know that when we are lonely or saddened by this world,
your heart also breaks.
Remind us that like Joseph and his brothers,
you too weep with us. And so we say to you, our dearest friend,
O God, we call.

Sometimes, God, we know we are slow to forgive others and that we hold grudges for too long. Help us to let go of bitterness that is in our hearts and help us to be open to the ways you are calling us to show mercy and grace to each other.
We know that there are people in our communities and in our world who are suffering from physical pains as well as pains of the heart. Help us to know how to help. And help us to know that our prayers, our care, and our presence is often better than letting things be left at arm's length.
And so we say to you, our dearest friend,
O God, we call.

We each have spaces in our own lives in which we are longing for forgiveness from you, O God. Help us in the silence of our hearts to now name our deepest longings and prayers. *(Silence.)* We gather all of these prayers, both spoken and in silence, and we say to you, our dearest friend,
O God, we call.
Amen.

***

We leave this place to encounter the Unknown,
attentive to the hints of holy
in glances and averted eyes,
smiles and frowns,
restful hands and shaky hands,
laughing and weeping,
leaving and coming back.
May the God of all Israel's children
and all the children of the earth
be with us as we go.

Sunday between August 21 and August 27 inclusive

Proper 16 [21]

LECTIONARY READINGS
Exodus 1:8—2:10
Psalm 124
Romans 12:1–8
Matthew 16:13–20

God of loving kindness and inspiring courage, we see your vision for just relations between people and nations. Sanctify our hospitality to strangers. Inspire our resistance against oppression. Enable our advocacy. Sustain our struggle. Amen.

***

We come together on the edge of possibilities.
For in this time, among this community,
we encounter Sacred Spirit who
awakens,
stirs,
convicts,
comforts,
renews,
transforms.
We come,
we gather,
we are open,
we wait…
(silence)

***

For times and ways we have closed our eyes
to the possibilities for transformation
within our neighbourhoods, our nation,
and the world we pray:
Bring us new sight. *(silence)*

For times and ways we have closed our hearts
to the opportunities for renewal
within ourselves and within our church we pray:
Reshape our hearts. *(silence)*

For times and ways we have held back our gifts
or resisted the gifts others would bring we pray:
Give us courage and grace. *(silence)*

***

O God of liberation, you call us to take action, and to live in the world – a world of brokenness and pain. We thank you for all those who act on behalf of others; we thank you for those who use the gifts you have given to do your will. May they inspire us to live into your call to take action. Amen.

***

One: Sometimes we fail to say "No"
to those who demand of us things that are contrary to your will.
All: **Forgive us.**
One: Sometimes we fail to say "Yes"
to risks that require faith that we have not yet acquired.
All: **Forgive us.**
One: Sometimes we fail to wait
for you to create a seemingly impossible opportunity for hope,
when all hope is lost.
All: **Forgive us.**

***

One: Though we may falter,
God's steadfast love is always ready to hold and support us.
All: **We are forgiven by God's grace; thanks be to God.**
Amen.

Sunday between August 28 and September 3 inclusive

Proper 17 [22]

LECTIONARY READINGS

Exodus 3:1–15
Psalm 105:1–6, 23–26, 45c
Romans 12:9–21
Matthew 16:21–28

Compassionate, loving God, every day we see and hear the misery and suffering of oppressed people. Too often, we do not know ourselves to be your partner in their liberation. Call us. Empower us. Consecrate us. Send us. Amen.

***

One: Love's strong voice calls us to move
beyond all that divides us, one from another.
Come, let us follow Love's lead.
Two: With generous grace,
love welcomes all that we are.
Come, let us follow Love's lead.
Three: Love invites us to be enfolded
into a community of mutual affection and respect.
Come, let us follow Love's lead.
Four: Love's tender voice stirs within us
a desire for harmony and peace.
Come, let us follow Love's lead.
Five: Love makes us kin with all in Christ
and reveals how we are to live together.
Come, let us follow Love's lead.
Six: Love creates space for worship
so we can rest in Sabbath's time.
Come, let us follow Love's lead.

***

Invite people to breathe in when they hear the words, "Genuine love," symbolic of taking in the loving ways, as the paraphrase of verses from Romans 12 is read. Then breathe out when they hear the word "Yet," symbolic of the attitudes and actions that actually get expressed at times.

(Breathe in.)
Genuine love holds fast to all that is good.
(Breathe out.)
Yet we sometimes cling
to resentments, judgments, and negativity.
(silent reflection)

(Breathe in.)
Genuine love strives to be mutual,
bringing honour to one another.
(Breathe out.)
Yet we can be demanding, self-serving, and demeaning at times.
(silent reflection)

(Breathe in.)
Genuine love seeks to welcome all
into the circle of love.
(Breathe out.)
Yet we often include only those
in whose circles we comfortably travel.
(silent reflection)

***

Love is merciful and forgiving.
Love ennobles and transforms.
Love makes it possible to overcome
every shortcoming with good.
Let us follow Love's lead
and be shaped into a community of faith.
Amen. Let it be so.

***

Who are we,
to offer praise to you, God,
when we often call on your name in vain?
Although we lack the words to describe our gratitude for all that you have given us,
we know that it is good to praise you.
So we offer our thanks to you now, both silently and aloud…
(Share joys within your community, or invite people to offer their prayers of thanksgiving.)

Who are we,
to offer our concerns for others,
when what we think they need is not what they truly need,
and our inability to provide comfort and peace scares us?
Although we may not know what to pray, we offer our prayers of concern to you,
knowing that the Spirit will intercede on our behalf…
(Share intercessory prayers.)

Who are we,
to offer prayers to you, God?
We are your children.
Your beloved.
So with confidence we share with you our prayers for ourselves and our ministries,
knowing that you will cherish our prayers as precious offerings…
(Share prayers of supplication.)

Who are you, God,
to hear and receive these prayers?
You are the great I AM.
You have journeyed with our ancestors as you continue to journey with us.
You are who you will be;
our creator, redeemer, and sustainer always.
Amen.

***

May the Holy Spirit light a fire within your heart: a fire that burns hot and bright, but that does not consume; a fire that illumines your path, without scorching the eye.
May the Holy Comforter journey with you: pouring the waters of welcome over your tired feet, and sharing the feast of love, bread, and wine for the journey.
May the Great Creator sustain you: smoothing out narrow and bumpy roads, to lovingly guide your pathway home.

Sunday between September 4 and September 10 inclusive

Proper 18 [23]

LECTIONARY READINGS
Exodus 12:1–14
Psalm 149
Romans 13:8–14
Matthew 18:15–20

Soil of life, our roots sink into you.
Water of life, our bodies thirst for you.
Light of life, our branches reach to you.
Breath of life, our fullness opens to you.
Mystery of life, our spirits rise in you.
Amen.

***

Great Restorer of Life,
we get disappointed when we try to understand
who we are by the things we accomplish
or the things we own or the labels others give us.
So we return to you and ask you to give us
a sense of what you have created us to be.
Help us find a common identity
in the stories of your powerful works
so that we can remind one another
of who we are in your name.

***

You are the One who made us all,
who made us whole,
so why do we live as though we are self-made,
and in doing so, move to brokenness:
within ourselves,
with others,
and with the world around us?

You are the One who made us –
wonderfully and in mystery –
so why do we settle for something less than awe
for ourselves and others?

Restore in us your Spirit,
that we may share life and breath with all creation.
This we pray in the name of Christ,
who spoke of such wonder,
in the birth of Spirit's new life.
Amen.

***

Like the tree whose roots
go beneath the surface, beyond our sight;
like that tree through which
water flows in and then out;
so is the assurance of God's love that holds us.
It is love that goes deep, anchoring us securely.
It is love that flows freely, bearing life to and from us.
Thanks be to God.

***

A bidding prayer is part of the Anglican/Church of England tradition, and is usually offered before the sermon. It is now often a part of other traditions and may be used as prayers of intercession or prayers of the people. In a "bidding prayer" an issue of concern or general need is identified and people are invited to offer their own prayers in silence. It may include a simple response, such as, "In your mercy, God of Life, ***Hear our prayer.****" You may introduce by saying:*
In space and silence let us pray today for the concerns that are on our hearts and minds as we encounter the One who loves this world and all within it.

Let us pray for…
The world in which we live.

(A silence is kept. Response, optional.)
People who have lost the capacity for awe and wonder.
(A silence is kept. Response, optional.)
A sense of the "unknown god" already in the world creating opportunities for discovery.
(A silence is kept. Response, optional.)
For world environments

> Major world forest areas
> Communities and companies dependent on the health of the forests
> Decision-makers responsible for decisions about environmental care
> Soils, plant varieties and animal life dependent on the health of forests with no voice with which to speak.

(A silence is kept. Response, optional.)
Indigenous people and cultures whose stories tell also of the wonder of creation, forests, rivers, land, and all the creatures of the earth.
(A silence is kept. Response, optional.)
Communities in conflict.
(A silence is kept. Response, optional.)
Communities of faith for courage, commitment, and compassion to care.
(A silence is kept. Response, optional.)

All: **Creating God, in whom we live and move, and have our being, tune our lives to your wonder and mystery. Amen.**

***

God of mystery, no longer unknown, you invite us to open conversations, discern connections, and seek always to develop relationships and communities of life and hope.
We align our lives with your love for the whole world, and join our longing with your desire for all generations to live, move, and be in you.
Amen.

***

You are a sign of God's freedom.
Go now in the Spirit of God.
Create a holy place wherever you go.
You are a sign of God's freedom.

Sunday between September 11 and September 17 inclusive

Proper 19 [24]

LECTIONARY READINGS

Exodus 14:19–31
Psalm 114 *or* Exodus 15:1b–11, 20–21
Romans 14:1–12
Matthew 18:21–35

In soil bringing seeds to life, in rocks holding the mysteries of time, in prairies alive with wind-blown grain, in mountains holding hearts on high: You, Holy One, are present. You are the life of all life, and all creation is blessed. Amen.

***

Hear our prayers, O God, for all grieved by death – whether a loved one held dear, or strangers we have never met who have perished in conflicts or natural disasters. We pray for comfort and strength as remains are returned to the earth in hopes that life will be drawn up from the earth as you have in Christ.

Hear our prayers, O God, for all who wander across many lands in search of home. For refugees fleeing war or famine; for the homeless, cast off by loss of job, or struggles with mental illness. May our prayers for such ones be joined in commitment to minister to and with them.

Hear our prayers, O God, for all who work to protect Earth against the ravages of natural disaster, or greed-driven indifference, or acts of violence in warfare without regard for what becomes of Earth beneath the weapons and the destruction and the chemicals. Stir in us a willingness to speak and act beyond the safety of study groups for the sake of your good creation.

Hear our prayers, O God, for the faithfulness of the church. For the church, too, is caretaker of the land we hold – even as we are called to be harbingers of the land and realm you promise. May our practices of and relationships with land, as individuals and congregations, be in keeping with the values of your commonwealth.

Hear our prayer, O God, for eyes and spirits open to your presence – especially in the places where we may feel you distant or removed, even in the places where we might try to flee from you. Even in those shadowed lands, you accompany us upon the way. You bring healing. You wait upon us. You love us with a love that will not let us go.

***

When we participate in ways that hurt others
even while we strive for freedom, restore us.
May we trust in your power more than in ourselves.
When we ignore voices that don't agree with us
even as we seek to hear calls for justice and hope, give us courage.
May we trust in your power more than in ourselves.
When we quietly or not so quietly rejoice
in violence or in the ruin of enemies
or the hurt of the one who hurts, return us to mercy.
May we trust in your power more than in ourselves.
When we cannot find within us
the capacity to forgive others
while we hope for forgiveness for ourselves,
abide with us in our struggle.
May we trust in your power more than in ourselves.

***

God's mercy as well as God's power are true.
God will grant us courage, mercy,
and a constant presence
in the midst of our shortcomings.
Believe in the good news:
We are forgiven and renewed
to live fully in God's ways.

***

All: **From many different lands we gather on this land, in this place, at this time.**
You are with us, God of the earth, the land, the sky.

One: In difficult times,
in difficult places,
in strange and unknown lands,
people gather to worship God in spirit and truth
and God is always here…
always near…
watching…
waiting…
listening…
breathing…
in spirit and in truth.

***

One: We are dust.
Two: We shall return to dust.

One: The land is filled with treasure.
Two: We have taken treasure from the land, and left it broken.

One: The land is rich to nourish and sustain.
Two: We strip it of goodness, turning fertile plains into wastelands.

One: The land is plentiful and full of variety.
Two: We fight for control, from desire for more,
it becomes killing-fields instead of sanctuary.

One & Two: The land cries out in agony, and the people cry out in misery.

One: The land longs for mercy,
Two: and the people yearn for comfort and care.

One & Two: God, are you there? Do you care?
Silence.

***

One: Even where the consequences for wrong are almost beyond enduring, there is no one and nowhere outside or beyond the reach of God's care. God's loving grace is abundant. God's gift of forgiveness opens the way for transformation and life.

All: **Thanks be to God, for the possibility of love.**

***

One: What can we offer,
what can we bring?

All: **You are the ground of everything:**
the source of all that is;
the hope on which we stand;
the promise that reaches out an open hand
and leads and holds us fast.
We bring our hopes, our dreams, our fears.
We bring our hands, our hearts, our tears. Amen.

***

Go from this place into the land beloved of God.
Tread lightly on the land, that your footprints may not harm.
Touch gently with your hands, that healing may bring hope.
Tremble softly in anticipation of the Spirit's presence,
transforming life with love in every time and place.

Sunday between September 18 and September 24 inclusive

Proper 20 [25]

LECTIONARY READINGS
Exodus 16:2–15
Psalm 105:1–6, 37–45
Philippians 1:21–30
Matthew 20:1–16

Spirit of Wilderness, we know about control; show us the letting go. We know about gardens; lead us to wildness. We know about full; empty us to spacious. We know about words; open us to your sighing. In your time and wisdom, may it be. Amen.

***

Dare we venture into the wild places?

Wilderness spaces –
frozen tundra,
windswept outback,
tangled bush,
jagged mountain ranges,
fathomless seas –
so much beauty, so much danger, so much uncertainty.

Dare we find God present?

In painful distress,
disappointed hopes,
and almost abandoned dreams,
Listen for the deep and anguished sighs and groans.

Yes, God, you are here!
Amen.

***

Invite people to close their fists as the leader prays and then open them during their spoken response.

God, when we get afraid of what lies ahead,
we want to go back to the old ways
instead of seeking your new way with us. *(silence)*
Forgive us and open us to you.
Holy Giver, our hands are open to receive your gifts.
When we don't see the signs of hope we expect,
we complain, we turn to other things,
and we blame each other. *(silence)*
Forgive us and open us to you.
Holy Giver, our hands are open to receive your gifts.
When we do have enough, we want even more
and, by wanting more,
often others have less than enough. *(silence)*
Forgive us and open us to you.
Holy Giver, our hands are open to receive your gifts.
When we work so hard to get something,
we forget your goodness and think our lives
are what we've done, have, or achieve. *(silence)*
Forgive us and open us to you.
Holy Giver, our hands are open to receive your gifts.

***

Our God is gracious and merciful,
slow to anger and abounding in steadfast love.
Trust in God's forgiveness and power
to transform our regret to mercy.

***

To you, O God, we pray
for ourselves: for forgiveness and for turning.
To you, O God, we pray
for and with the wild places:
for healing, for restoration.

To you, O God, we pray
for awe and wonder in our world and in our lives.

***

You lead us to a time and place apart, O God, for prayer. Prayer that does not seek escape from the world and the wild places, but rather for healing and redemptive actions within it.

Your Spirit prays, and we long, for peace: in the midst of conflicts and hatreds, from lusting for power and wealth. Use your impatience to spur just action, and our patience to hold steady over the long course.

Your Spirit prays, and we long, for creation's renewal: in the face of declining habitats and wild places, from lusting to control and usurp. Remind us of the integrity of all creation in you, that we not sell out or settle for divide and conquer, or close our eyes to the causes of destructive climate change.

Your Spirit prays, and we long, for justice and a just sharing of what makes for life: food and water, hope and love, justice and mercy, wild places and sanctuaries.

Your Spirit prays, and we long, for the caring for vulnerable ones: that they may not go forgotten or without advocates.

Your Spirit prays, and we long, for coming generations: that our children and children's children may know they are loved by us as well as you; and that such love be embodied by our passing on of wild places intact.

Your Spirit prays, and we long, for your realm brought to earth: and in such longing and prayer, we open ourselves to your leading, for the sake of your new creation. Amen.

Sunday between September 25 and October 1 inclusive

Proper 21 [26]

LECTIONARY READINGS

Exodus 17:1–7
Psalm 78:1–4, 12–16
Philippians 2:1–13
Matthew 21:23–32

Ring a chime, play a singing bowl, or sound a rain stick during this call to worship.

When we are hungry for a sustaining faith, we ask,
Are you among us, O God?
(Sound an instrument.)
When we are thirsty for justice and peace, we ask,
Are you among us, O God?
(Sound an instrument.)
As wandering people who long for mercy, we ask,
Are you among us, O God?
(Sound an instrument.)
Secure in the freedom of your love, we ask,
Are you among us, O God?
(Sound an instrument.)

***

Slowly fill the baptismal font or bowl using a pitcher of water as the prayer is offered. If necessary, position a microphone near the bowl/font so that the sound of water flowing is clearly heard.

In holy presence we gather.
We move into the waters of God:
deep silent pools,
loud rushing rapids,
strong steady rivers –
as those whose life flows from God.

We lift our voice with the voice of rivers:
acknowledging our many sources,
seeking outlets for sharing our gifts,
borne up by the current of Spirit toward hope.

We listen with the waters
for covenanted words and signs,
that we may trust and work toward
God's promises with courage freed from fear.
In holy presence,
immersed in holy waters,
we gather to worship.

***

God, the water of life, we acknowledge the importance of water in the maintenance and operation of creation and how it is vital to our lives. Guide us in the responsible use of and respect for water around the world. Amen.

***

Pour half of a glass of water into a jug of water.

One: When we are empty,
All: **fill us, O God.**
One: When we are careless,
All: **wash us clean.**
One: When we are selfish,
All: **spill over our edges.**
One: When we are frightened,
All: **ripple in gentle pools.**
One: When we are dry,
All: **rain in our hearts.**
One: When we are bogged down,
All: **set your rainbow above us.**
One: When we are asleep,
All: **splash us awake with crystal clear droplets.**

For we forget our call
to let your healing waters flow through us. Amen.

***

God rains down manna in the wilderness
and squeezes water from a desert rock.
With fire and cloud God leads us
out of the bondage of our past
into a future of freedom and safety.
God has been with us in the past,
is with us in this present moment,
and will be with us forever and ever.

***

Creator God,
Mysterious as the essence of life, there is hope and healing at the core of life.
Expand our awareness of the hurts and hopes of the world around us,
Arouse us, God of the life-giving river, to serve and to care.
Nations struggle together and internally, erupting in violence,
polluting rivers and streams, destroying land
and leaving the lives of their people in ruins… *(name places of particular concern).*
Inspire within us hearts and minds of deep compassion
that we may not be idle, paddling our feet, or watering our vegetable gardens
while people are hungry for food and for love… *(name situations of particular concern).*
Nurture within us a sense that the time is now,
to look beyond our own fears,
and share with those who have grasped already
the urgent need to heal the Earth… *(name ways in which your community acts to heal).*
Grow us in wisdom, knowledge, and love
that we may be like trees bearing fruit and providing for the healing of the nations

from the life-giving core of our lives.
Amen.

***

Play the chime, singing bowl, or rain stick.

You have watered our desert souls.
(Sound an instrument.)
We cried out in our longings and you answered.
(Sound an instrument.)
You drew near to us bringing comfort and peace.
(Sound an instrument.)
We leave now with the assurance of your presence
always with us, in and around us,
the sturdy rock upon which we stand.
(Sound an instrument.)

Sunday between October 2 and October 8 inclusive

Proper 22 [27]

LECTIONARY READINGS
Exodus 20:1–4, 7–9, 12–20
Psalm 19
Philippians 3:4b–14
Matthew 21:33–46

O God, we come seeking wisdom for the way.
Plant the seed of your law in our hearts where it may be nourished with the story of your faithful people and take root in our lives.

***

Arrange to have four people stand in the four corners of the worship space. The readers will take turns saying one of the words from each of the lists of words of contemplation below. Follow each word with ample silence. Explain that rather than speaking a prayer with prescribed sentences and thoughts, we will hear single words. Invite those gathered to be attentive to the thoughts and feelings that arise with each word and allow these responses to guide a silent prayer of confession.

Distance, separation, division, broken-hearted
(give ample pause between each word);

Harm, neglect, pollution, extinction
(give ample pause between each word);

Disregard, ignore, injustice, impoverish
(give ample pause between each word).

***

Have the four people who read the words continue reading the words below slowly, but without the extended space for silent prayer.

Hear now these life-giving words:
receive, welcome, reconcile, enfold;
restore, conserve, beautify, care;
attend, share, compassion, love;
forgiven, forgiven, forgiven, forgiven.

May these words take root within us and become the living reality among and through us.

***

God, in your mercy help us to find the courage to learn from the experiences of the people of Israel as they journeyed toward freedom, and wisdom so we may find commonality with our own journey – both in the body and in the Spirit. Amen.

***

One: Many of us struggle with feelings of failure because we have not lived up to our own or others' expectations.
God's realm embraces the spirit rather than the letter of the Law. God gives life rather than condemnation.
In this confidence, we open ourselves to God. Let us pray.
When we are afraid that we do not live up to expectations,
when we become overwrought with our shortcomings,
All: **calm our anxious hearts, O God.**

One: When we feel so angry that we effectively murder relationships and break the bonds of community with malice,
All: **stir our memories of love for one another, O God.**

One: When we are caught in the little white lies that tangle us almost imperceptibly into ever-tightening webs of deceit,
All: **give us courage to carry the truth, O God.**

One: When our lives are so packed full that we barely have time to breathe;
or succumb to things that glitter and consume our energy to attain,

All: **shift our focus to your delight, O God. Amen.**

***

One: Friends; long ago, Moses reminded the people that they did not need to be afraid of God. Rather, they were invited into a transformed way of living, guided by the One who is able to make all things new.
Let Christ be your example and your goal, and the spirit of the law your guide.
You are forgiven.

All: **We will press on in the Spirit toward the life made perfect through Christ who fulfills the law and sets us free.**

***

One: God, you are the essence of life,
And you long for all people to share in the goodness you offer.
As we learn to live in the power of your sweet Spirit, we are so aware of a beautiful world torn apart by all those things addressed in your precious law.

We pray for people whose lives have been shattered by the anger, malice, and destructiveness that murders relationships…

We pray for communities, countries, and cultures afflicted by the ravages of war, greed, intolerance, and oppression…

We pray for homes and families struggling with the demands of employment, and the expectations of success constantly demanding attention…

We pray for people who are seeking to forge new relationships, venturing into uncertain territory, and wondering how they will shape their futures in ways that bring hope to the land…

We pray for people who are learning to live with enough, daring to resist the endless expectations for more, and working for the common good of even those who rebuke and ridicule…

We pray for those quiet, persistent voices that remind us all that there is a language of the Cosmos inviting hope, and stirring the precious life within toward a holy wholeness…

All: **Holy One, may we be the people who cultivate kindness, stir the embers of truth, and listen in the silence for your voice.**

One: May we be people attentive to care, who discern the spirit of the law that brings freedom to live and life for all.
Let it be so. Amen.

***

Go with ways of wisdom for the Holy One:
faithfulness,
loyalty,
reverence,
stillness,
respect.

Go with ways of wisdom for community:
mutuality,
honour,
generosity,
truthfulness,
contentment.

Go in the wisdom of Christ that enables all creation to flourish in the ways of love:
forgiving,
healing,
restoring,
creating,
life.

Sunday between October 9 and October 15 inclusive

Proper 23 [28]

LECTIONARY READINGS

Exodus 32:1–14
Psalm 106:1–6, 19–23
Philippians 4:1–9
Matthew 22:1–14

God of mighty deeds and gentle mercies,
we gather to give you praise this day.
We join with all of creation
in uttering our small words of thanks
for your steadfast love which endures forever.
May our very lives be lived as a song of praise
to you, the God of our salvation.

***

One: We emerge cautiously, to expose our deepest thoughts, anxieties, and fears to God.

Two: When I cannot see you, God, I long for something visible to prove you are real and true.

Three: When those who lead in your name disappoint, disappear or argue bitterly, I feel abandoned, betrayed, and confused.

Four: When my questions reverberate as if unheard, I feel uncertain, afraid, and foolish.

One: When the way ahead seems so uncertain, we attach ourselves to those who are confident and sure.

Two: When life is unendingly difficult, we seek happiness and comfort in the world around us.

Three: When the journey is so lonely, we turn back to the familiar ways we have always known.

Together: Your time is not our time, God.
We do not know the way ahead.
We want clarity and security…
and yet, much more, we want to live…

Pause.

One: We are emerging into the light of the one who knows our frailties, our weakness, our wavering…and loves beyond all measure. God's peace surpasses our worry and uncertainty. God's peace will guide our hearts and minds into the ways of life in Christ.

All: **We will risk letting go and trust God to guide us on the way.**

***

One: God does not seek our offerings of gold or finest robes.

All: **We do not want to be distracted**
by what we have, what we wear,
or any other symbols of success and importance in our culture,
and so we offer all these things and our whole selves
in joy and trust
as we step into the journey with God.

One: God seeks the turning of our lives in ways that lead to life for all.

All: **We bring what we have and who we are**
that we may be a life-bringing voice,
and a sign of hope and peace for a world in need.
Amen.

***

One: Whatever is true,
whatever is honourable,
whatever is just:

Two: remember these things!

All: **Do these things!**

One: Whatever is pure,
whatever is pleasing,
whatever is commendable:

Two: Remember these things!

All: **Do these things!**

One: Rejoice in God.
Two: Help one another.
All: **Trust that the peace of God,**
which surpasses all understanding,
will keep our hearts and minds in Christ Jesus.

Sunday between October 16 and October 22 inclusive

Proper 24 [29]

LECTIONARY READINGS
Exodus 33:12–23
Psalm 99
1 Thessalonians 1:1–10
Matthew 22:15–22

Voice One stands at the front of the worship space while Voice Two is clearly heard but not seen.

One: In this sacred place we leave behind
the world of thoughtless unanimity
and we hear the voice of God say to each one of us,
Two: I know you by name.
All: **Show us your glory, O God.**

One: In this sacred place we encounter sign and symbol
in font and pulpit, bread broken and shared,
and we hear the voice of God say to us,
Two: My presence goes with you, and I will give you rest.
All: **Show us your glory, O God.**

One: In this sacred place we give thanks
for this community of faith bound together
by a common ministry and affirmed by God who says,
Two: You have found favour in my sight.
All: **Show us your glory, O God.**

***

A steady heartbeat sounds quietly beneath the spoken words of this prayer.

One: Ah, God of every moment and every day,
you are more real to us than our breathing,
more constant than our heartbeat,
more present to us than our senses,

yet more mysterious than we can comprehend.
Two: Dare we ask that your presence be known among us?
One: In justice, fairness, and goodness,
and where wrongs are put right
we know you are near.
Two: Love and gentleness, kindness and courage
imprint your image on every part of life,
and we know you are near.
All: **We praise you.**
We listen for you.
We attend to your pulse in the whole of life. Amen.

***

God of glory, you call us by name and shape us into a living message. Affirm your presence in our lives and in this, your community, so we can become strong and faithful witnesses to your way in this world.

***

Create a slide show – take pictures of people in your congregation engaged in different ministries such as teaching, serving at a food bank, and visiting others at home. Include photos of nature and neighbourhood life also. Play the slide show during the prayer.

All living things imitate God.
As flowers bloom, as trees bear fruit,
as dancers leap high in air,
they imitate your creativity, O God.

As we struggle for justice,
as we resolve conflict through peace,
as we extend our hand to our neighbour,
we imitate your love, O God.

As we stand firm in our faith,
as we teach and nurture our children,
as we pray for our world,
we imitate your love, O God.

So we give thanks to you, O God,
for your goodness
which is in our hearts and minds
in our strength and soul
in our life and love.
Praise be to you, O God. Amen.

***

Holy Companion, the place I will not go is the one where you are not. The rock I will not hold is the one you will not pass. The rest I will not have is the one you have not given. The friendship I will not live is the one that is not of you. Amen.

***

This is from an ancient Celtic confessional song, attributed to St. Patrick, expressing the Christ who is present everywhere.

Christ be with me, Christ within me,
Christ behind me, Christ before me,
Christ beside me, Christ to win me,
Christ to comfort and restore me,
Christ beneath me, Christ above me,
Christ in quiet, Christ in danger,
Christ in hearts of all who love me,
Christ in mouth of friends and stranger.

***

Go boldly into the world.
Go seek out new ways to be God's holy ones.
Go into the world with God's good news.
You are the message.
Be the message.
Do the message.
Live the message.

As you go the love of God, the grace of Jesus Christ,
and the inspiration of the Holy Spirit go with you.
Thanks be to God.

Sunday between October 23 and October 29 inclusive

Proper 25 [30]

LECTIONARY READINGS

Deuteronomy 34:1–12
Psalm 90:1–6, 13–17
1 Thessalonians 2:1–8
Matthew 22:34–46

Love God with all your heart *(gesture to heart).*
Love your neighbour as yourself.
Love God with all your mind *(gesture to head).*
Love your neighbour as yourself.
Love God with all your strength *(make a muscle).*
Love your neighbour as yourself.
We worship God with our whole being *(designate whole body).*
Love your neighbour as yourself.

***

God, when we stand at the edge of brokenness
and allow our questions of faith
to distance ourselves from you and others,
forgive us and free us.
When the ways we live church
limit our ability to offer compassion,
forgive us and free us.
When we try to be holy
without changing the way we are with others,
forgive us and free us.

***

The face of God we seek is a face of compassion,
steadfast in love, and longing to forgive.
Receive the power of God's compassion
so that we might have the capacity for love.

***

One: Think about the endings and beginnings in your lives. This may not be easy. There are many painful experiences from which we carry the sadness and scars. Yet God is with us in all these moments.

Take a deep breath, hold it for the count of four, and slowly let it go.

Continue to take a deep breath in and slowly release as each part of the prayer is led. It may help to take a new breath at the word "sometimes…"

Sometimes we are afraid of change, God.
It makes us feel uncomfortable and wary, and we resent those who suggest its benefit.
Pause.

Sometimes, we hold grudges from old arguments or differences of opinion.
We prefer to break a relationship than let go.
Pause.

Sometimes, we hold on to our grieving and do not let it out.
We are afraid that everything we have valued will unravel.
Pause.

Sometimes, when you call us into freedom, we hanker for the safety of what we have known; we bury ourselves in debates and questions, rather than risk acting as if we were free.
Pause.

Sometimes, God, we would let it out.
Help us let go, God.
Set us free.
Amen.

***

New beginnings continue,
for we live and move and have our being
in God's unfolding story.
Fresh choices continue,
for we live and move and have our being
in God's unfolding story.
We will be remembered,
for we live in God's unfolding story.
Thanks be to God,
the dwelling place of all generations.

***

One: God of our journey,
God who is present with us at all times,
God who leads and guides and comes amongst us in word, and wisdom,
in spirit, love, and life,
there have been many endings and beginnings in our personal and communal journeys.

For all the endings in our lives,
no matter how hard they have been,
we dare to thank you.
As a community we have struggled with many things,
yet we have learned so much,
and seek your presence with us
into the future.

All: **We seek to be a people who bring honour to you as we live in the courage, persistence, and truthfulness that we have learned from Christ, and those who have followed wisely in Christ's way.**

One: We pray that we will be compassionate advocates standing

with those who struggle to find a place, with those who do not sense a future, with those who are insecure, with those who have been hurt and broken.
We pray that we will be just in our actions and that our words may match our deeds in kindness.
We pray that we will recognize your wise guides, and be honest in our learning.
We trust that you will be in each of our beginnings as community.

All: **We pray in the name of Jesus the Christ**
who has shown the depth of love for friend and stranger
and whose ending is our beginning, forever. Amen.

***

In Deuteronomy, the story of Moses unfolded into the story of Joshua.
In God, even our endings find new beginnings.
For God is the One in whom all dwell,
and God's story goes on.

Sunday between October 30 and November 5 inclusive

Proper 26 [31]

LECTIONARY READINGS
Joshua 3:7–17
Psalm 107:1–7, 33–37
1 Thessalonians 2:9–13
Matthew 23:1–12

Gracious God, you have told us what is good. Jesus has shown us what you require of us: to do justice, to love kindness, and to walk humbly with you. Enliven our spirits with your Spirit to love you more dearly and to serve you more fully. Amen.

***

Come as the gathered of God,
brought into God's storied presence and saving love.
Give thanks to God,
whose steadfast love endures forever.
Come from and with your wanderings and searchings.
Give thanks to God, who companions us on our way.
Come with your thirst and hunger for that which is good, and that which brings good.
Give thanks to God, whose goodness does not fail.
Come as those who would be
encouraged and transformed by God.
Give thanks to God,
whose purpose is life renewed and redeemed.

***

Gracious God,
we acknowledge that in the actions we have displayed
we may have forgotten you in these moments.
There are times when we congratulate ourselves,
forgetting your guiding role in what we achieved.

We acknowledge that in the events in which we have participated,
we have hurt others, ignoring their needs and putting ourselves first.

May we remember that we are created to live in community with you
and all creation.

In all our actions, God, may we remember to serve you wholeheartedly;
not saying one thing, and acting on another.

May we have the courage to admit when we let pride rule,
and act humbly as we serve. Amen.

***

One: God invites us to participate,
calls us to share,
and draws us together as one.
All: **For your trust in us, we thank you, God. Amen.**

***

Merciful One,
you bring light to our shadowed existence,
you offer satisfaction to our hunger,
you give hope to our despair.
God, your steadfast love endures forever.

Merciful One,
you free us from burdens we carry –
our sadness and mourning,
our sense of not being up to the job –
by reminding us that we are not alone.
God, your steadfast love endures forever.

Merciful One,
teach us as the church to lift up your promises
by our joyful struggle with scripture,
by our songs and prayers,

by our care of one another,
and our ministry in the world.
God, your steadfast love endures forever.

Merciful One,
teach us to ask for help and receive care
when it feels like we carry too much on our own.
God, your steadfast love endures forever.

Merciful One,
teach us the ways to encourage one another
and take notice of your glory
in the words and actions of one another.
God, your steadfast love endures forever.

Merciful One,
teach our world to satisfy the thirsty, the hungry, and hopeless.
God, your steadfast love endures forever.

***

One: May we be mindful in the things that we say.
May we be mindful in the actions we do.

All: Let us remember to set your will first.
Let us remember in the actions we do.

One: Help us to recognize God through, with, and in people.
Help us to recognize in the actions we do.

All: In remembering, recognizing, and mindfulness,
we will serve you, God, through our actions and our words.
Amen.

***

Those whom God has gathered, God now sends forth.
We are blessed to go
in the presence of God who leads us.
As long as we follow in the way God is leading –
we know God's realm will surely appear.
Go then as the people of God,
encouraged and empowered
by God who goes with us.

Sunday between November 6 and November 12 inclusive

Proper 27 [32]

LECTIONARY READINGS
Joshua 24:1–3a, 14–25
Psalm 78:1–7
1 Thessalonians 4:13–18
Matthew 25:1–13

Gathered together
we look for what will be.
Expecting to worship
we settle our bodies and still our minds.

Feeling our hearts beat
we know our own potential.
Alive to all that is around us
we are awake to possibilities.

The Spirit is gently moving
we become a worshipping community.
We are ready to pray, to sing, to listen
we are ready to worship.

***

Help us this day, O God, to receive the gift of your word with joy; make our hearts long for closeness with you. Be our ever-present guide as we live toward your purpose and shine as witnesses to your grace and justice. Amen.

***

Grant us, O God, life in the light of faith, that we may be enlightened within, and bright and lively beacons without; that we may give illuminating and truthful witness to the brilliance of your grace and justice. This is our choice. Amen.

***

Have three oil lamps or large candles lit on the worship table.

Holy One, we move through our days
with dreams of your banquet of justice,
your everlasting honeymoon of inclusive community.
We give thanks for all the ways
you light our paths and keep us in the ways of hope.
We await the way of Love.
(Extinguish one lamp/candle.)

Yet the way of Love can be slow in coming.
We pray for our hearts
that can impatiently stretch ahead of us
with expectations of ourselves,
our community, and God's work within us.
We await the way of Love.
(Extinguish one lamp/candle.)

We are mindful of the troubling news of these days
that weighs on our minds and spirits.
We pray for all who long for peace with justice
in their relationships, their homeland,
in all the places of your creation.
We await the way of love.
(Extinguish one lamp/candle.)

***

May we be encouraged with these words:
God does not delay in responding
but is with us always and in every circumstance.
In every word of forgiveness –
there is God! *(Light one lamp/candle.)*
In every move toward greater compassion –
there is God! *(Light one lamp/candle.)*
In every act of justice –
there is God! *(Light one lamp/candle.)*

When we live the way of Love,
our world shines with the presence of God.
Thanks be to God.

***

One: Loving God, we give thanks for all the ways you light our path and keep us in the ways of hope.
All: **Guide us in your loving ways.**
One: We hope for those who have received or experienced troubling or joyful news in these days.
All: **Guide us in your loving ways.**
One: We pray for our own hearts that impatiently stretch ahead of us with expectations of ourselves, our community, and your holy work with us.
All: **Guide us in your loving ways.**
One: We pray for those awaiting release from prison, and those longing for a renewed sense of your presence.
All: **Guide us in your loving ways.**
One: We pray for all who await peace with justice in their relationships, in their homeland, in all the places of your creation.
All: **Guide us in your loving ways.**
Amen.

***

One: We are called to serve you, God,
and remain steady and certain on your word.
May we remain faithful,
full of endurance and hope in you.

God, we ask that you may fill us with patience.
Entrust us with your work to educate, participate,
and encourage others to become involved in your creation,
so we all may be a part of your glory.

One: God, we pray…
All: **Grant us wisdom as we seek to live in your way.**

***

We go forth into this day
with the glory of God's anticipation moving through us.
With active longing, we await inspiration,
clarity of purpose, and new gifts of the Spirit.
Go with the light of God,
the affirming love of Jesus Christ,
and the ever-renewing power of the Holy Spirit.

Sunday between November 13 and November 19 inclusive

Proper 28 [33]

LECTIONARY READINGS

Judges 4:1–7
Psalm 123
1 Thessalonians 5:1–11
Matthew 25:14–30

Extravagant, loving God, your grace saves, your compassion gives life, your justice restores.
Investing God, call us to risky adventures, to touch the lives of neighbours and strangers.
In faith, hope, and love, we risk our lives for yours. Amen.

***

Invite the gathered community to read this responsively.

One: We lift our eyes and raise our hearts and are met by the Holy One in worship.
Two: We stretch out our arms and open our hands in the hope of finding mercy.
One: In our stretching, we are met by the kind eyes and warm hands of companions on the way.
Two: May we be aware of the signs of love that are always with us.

***

Invite the people to watch and follow the actions of this prayer. As the response is a repeated one, practice it first so hands are free of bulletins.

(hands across their hearts)
One: Almighty God, you have created us as a people each with different gifts.
All: **Each an individual,**
all empowered to contribute in your world.

(holding the hands of those next to you)

One: You have created us, a people, to live in community.
**All: Each an individual,
all empowered to contribute in your world.**

(hands out palms facing up)

One: You have created us, a people, and given gifts with which to serve you.
**All: Each an individual,
all empowered to contribute in your world.**

(hands up, palms reaching out)

One: You have created us, and called us to serve.
**All: Each an individual,
all empowered to contribute in your world. Amen.**

***

Sometimes, we abandon our hopes, our dreams, our plans – and then get angry when things don't turn out as we had hoped.
Sometimes, we leave others in charge of things, and then put them down for how they took care of it.
Sometimes, we are greedy.
Sometimes, we give up.
In all these times, and more besides, forgive us, O God.
Your grace saves, your compassion gives life, your justice restores.
Investing God, call us to risky adventures, to touch the lives of neighbours and strangers.
In faith, hope, and love, we risk for you. Amen.

***

God has blessed each one with a unique way to contribute.
God offers grace, forgiveness, healing, freedom, talent, life, new life.
Let us embrace the life that God gives.

***

Gracious God,
for those moments when people feel like what they offer is never enough,
we pray that they may be filled with hope and strength to recognize and invest in their gifts.

We pray that those who have wealth, power, and political ties
may use their positions for the good of all.

We pray for people in situations of oppression,
where dignity and self-worth are violated, and where greed diminishes the life of another.

We pray for those in our community who are sick *(pause)*, depressed *(pause)*, mourning losses *(pause)*, seeking new hope *(pause)*, looking for work *(pause)*, or feeling alienated.

In all these things, grant us courage to respond with your gifts of mercy, encouragement, love, kindness, endurance. Amen.

***

Friends, go well,
with and within
the currents of Spirit.
Amen.

Be of good courage,
and gentle of heart.
Be of wise mind,
and open to new instruction.
Be of vision,
not ignoring the obvious and pressing.
Be of simple faith,
yet radically open to questions and doubts.
Be free;
a generous healing and freedom for others.

Reign of Christ or Christ the King Sunday

Proper 29 [34]

LECTIONARY READINGS
Ezekiel 34:11–16, 20–24
Psalm 100
Ephesians 1:15–23
Matthew 25:31–46

Encourage the congregation, or the children within the congregation, to give a joyful cheer, clap, or play a noisemaker at the end of each response.

Make a joyful noise to God, all the earth;
sing, shout, dance,
and worship with exclamation-mark faith!
We are God's people, hurray!
The Holy One is God,
the Holy One made us
and we are like sheep in God's sheepfold.
We are God's people, hurray!
Enter this sacred place with thanksgiving,
ready to give thanks
and to offer gratitude to God.
We are God's people, hurray!
For the Holy One is good
and steadfast love and faithfulness
will be God's nature forever.
We are God's people, hurray!

***

Joy-making, shepherding God, your love, goodness, mercy, and grace are constantly before us. May we know you so well that we implicitly trust you, and unselfconsciously live to your glory and praise. Amen.

***

Invite the people to pray with their hands open and their palms facing up.

Gracious God,
your people hunger and thirst each day,
through lack of food, or lack of spiritual nourishment.
Open us to recognize the ways you reveal your grace, your blessings,
and your comforting presence.

You are our guide,
revealing the path on which we are to travel.
Help us to see your presence in one another,
and make us ready to act lovingly,
openly,
honestly,
and humbly
in the way of Christ. Amen.

***

Tightly bound within familiar worlds
and too often sealed off from the worlds of others,
we now take our leave for a more fertile place:
We seek an openness of heart.
We seek the pulse of Spirit.
We seek an ability to perceive.
We seek the capacity to feel and to act with compassion for others
(pause for silence).

In your forgiveness, O God,
return us to broader perspectives
and a firmer courage to live in the realm of Christ.
We seek an openness of heart.
We seek the pulse of Spirit.
We seek an ability to see.
We seek the capacity to feel and to act with compassion for others
(pause for silence).
Amen.

***

Provide a moment to pass the peace after this prayer.

Friends, the grace and wisdom of God
always breaks open
new ways of being and doing.
It always gives rise to more generous
and fresh expressions of humanity.

So let us be a compassionate
and healing presence of Christ within the world.

***

One: For our sisters
All: **we pray peace.**
One: For our brothers,
All: **we pray peace.**

One: For our leaders,
All: **we pray peace.**

One: For the outcast,
All: **we pray peace.**

One: For your guidance in each day,
we pray for those we name *(name specific people/things).*
One: We pray for peace in all these we have spoken,
and whatever still lies on our hearts.
All: **We pray for peace in all things.**
Amen.

***

To be read either as a responsive prayer, or by two people.

One: May we respond to basic needs of life: food, water, shelter, love;
All: **and offer nourishment, warmth, shelter, protection.**

One: May we recognize the stranger,
All: **and offer friendship, kindness, and welcome.**
One: May we recognize the sick,
All: **and offer comfort, peace, and patience.**
One: May we recognize the imprisoned,
All: **and offer time, graciously, out of concern and love.**
May our gifts meet the longings of your people.
Amen.

***

Go forth and be the hand that heals
and the ears that listen with patience.
We are your people, O God.
Be the feet that stand with the oppressed
and the mouth that speaks truth.
We are your people, O God.
Be the eyes that see the holy in all people
and the heart that is full of life.
We are your people, O God.
Go now in peace and may the Spirit of Christ
reign in your hearts.

HEBREW SCRIPTURES INDEX

NEW TESTAMENT INDEX

Wood Lake

Imagining, living, and telling the faith story.

WOOD LAKE IS THE
FAITH STORY COMPANY.

It has told

• the story of the seasons of the earth, the people of God, and the place and purpose of faith in the world;

• the story of the faith journey, from birth to death;

• the story of Jesus and the churches that carry his message.

Wood Lake has been telling stories for more than 30 years. During that time, it has given form and substance to the words, songs, pictures, and ideas of hundreds of storytellers.

Those stories have taken a multitude of forms – parables, poems, drawings, prayers, epiphanies, songs, books, paintings, hymns, curricula – all driven by a common mission of serving those on the faith journey.